Running the Changes

The Definitive Guide to Jazz Improvisation for All Instruments

by Mike Steinel

Recording Personnel
Trumpet: Mike Steinel
Alto and Tenor Saxophone: Chris McGuire
Trombone: Tony Baker
Vocals: Rosana Eckert and Greg Jasperse
Piano: Mike Steinel
Guitar: Paul Metzger
Bass: Steve Heffner
Drums: Steve Barnes

Recorded at Reeltime Audio, Denton, TX
Recording and Mastering Engineer: Eric Delegard

PLAYBACK+
Speed • Pitch • Balance • Loop

To access audio visit:
www.halleonard.com/mylibrary

Enter Code
7001-4694-6046-1358

ISBN 978-1-70513-727-7

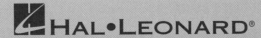

HAL•LEONARD®

Visit Hal Leonard Online at
www.halleonard.com

World headquarters, contact:
Hal Leonard
7777 West Bluemound Road
Milwaukee, WI 53213
Email: info@halleonard.com

In Europe, contact:
Hal Leonard Europe Limited
42 Wigmore Street
Marylebone, London, W1U 2RN
Email: info@halleonardeurope.com

In Australia, contact:
Hal Leonard Australia Pty. Ltd.
4 Lentara Court
Cheltenham, Victoria, 3192 Australia
Email: info@halleonard.com.au

Contents

Preface

There are many fine books available to jazz students today. Most focus on one topic, such as jazz history, jazz theory, instrumental technique, transcription analysis, or a specific improvisational device. It is easy to become overwhelmed and confused by the sheer volume and variety of information at times. It was not my intent to write another book that might add to the confusion, but instead, to produce a document that is concise, comprehensive, and comprehensible.

The idea for this book grew from a handout I prepared for an improvisation class in 2016. At that time, my teaching covered a wide range of topics but placed emphasis on the two basic strategies for negotiating changes (chord progressions) that I felt were the most helpful for the most students: ornamenting color tones and the "7-to-3" resolution. Worried that I might be leaving students with the impression that those were the only two ways to deal with harmony, I wrote a 12-page booklet: *A Concise Guide to Change Running*. That document listed and described nine unique improvisation strategies, each with its own advantages and disadvantages. Preparing it gave me new perspective on the history of jazz improvisation and how that history provides an outline of the basic skills an improviser needs and the best order in which to acquire them. *Running the Changes* is my attempt to present those common devices and techniques, explain why they are effective, show students how to practice them, and provide examples of their use over typical jazz progressions (changes). There is a certain amount of theory in some of the chapters, but *Running the Changes* is by no means a jazz theory text.

- Theory without application is useless.
- Technique without perspective is meaningless.

Theory is only included in this book to offer context and clarification to help students apply a particular approach characteristically. By that same token, the technique exercises are only included to build the necessary skill to execute those approaches with artistry.

The book's organization provides a step-by-step plan appropriate for both beginners and intermediate performers. After 40 years of attempting to teach jazz improvisation, I am, now more than ever, certain that to be successful teaching improvisation, we must: 1) Provide students with concepts that are valid (in other words, actually used by jazz musicians); 2) Show them how they can apply them to make jazz; and 3) Provide them the opportunities to explore and create. That is what I have attempted to do in *Running the Changes*.

Some of the topics in *Running the Changes* are worthy of more extensive study, and indeed, entire books have been written about many of those topics. When appropriate, I have suggested additional materials by other authors that provide more in-depth explorations.

Acknowledgments

I wish to thank my wife Beverly Hoch for her unwavering support. I also want to thank the great educators who have mentored me directly and indirectly in my career: Dan Haerle, Neil Slater, Jim Riggs, Jerry Coker, and David Baker. I owe a debt of gratitude to the many colleagues I have worked with at the University of North Texas for 32 years and to the thousands of talented students who have amazed me with their dedication to the art of jazz.

Introduction

"Change running," "running the changes," "making the changes," "making the harmony," and "achieving harmonic clarity" all refer to one basic goal: playing or singing improvised melodies that sound like the harmony (chord progression) and contain characteristic jazz rhythms. *Running the Changes* addresses that basic goal, in a comprehensive manner, by presenting strategies to accomplish accurate and artistic change running.

Some strategies in this book are more appropriate for beginners and can be put to use quickly. Others require more experience and practice. All of the techniques detailed in this book are contained in the solos of jazz masters. You don't need much experience to explore the concepts in this book—just the ability to read music and knowledge of major scales.

Modern jazz improvisations generally consist of single-note melodies performed with a rhythm section accompaniment, which usually includes a chording instrument (piano or guitar). *Running the Changes* focuses on this type of improvisation. It is important to note at this point, jazz solos, in the prevailing style today, contain two approaches to harmony: **inside playing** and **outside playing**.

Definitions

- **Inside Playing:** Improvised melodies that are consonant with the underlying harmony

- **Consonant:** "Sounds like the changes," "implies the changes," "fits with the changes," etc.

- **Outside Playing:** Improvising melodies that are dissonant with the underlying harmony

- **Dissonant:** "Sounds harsh," "doesn't agree or fit with the harmony," etc.

Although "inside" and "outside" improvisation may sound radically different, the ability to do both, with musicality, requires an understanding of harmony and the skill to manipulate note choices in real time. Some (the gifted few) may be able to play inside and outside at will, relying solely on a keen aural awareness, but most will need careful study and diligent practice to become proficient at either. Usually, mastery of "inside" playing precedes more advanced "outside" approaches. Eventually, an understanding of chord construction, chord function, scales, modes, and chord/scale relationships will help the improviser develop the link between the intellect (what we think), the ear (what we hear), and the body (what we feel when playing an instrument).

Running the Changes is based on a set of 12 principles:

Principle #1: Human Learning = Imitation + Exploration
Humans develop skills through **imitation and exploration**. Skills, acquired successfully, are the result of neurons in the brain connecting to other neurons to create **neural pathways**. Each neural pathway is a memory. When skills are repeated, they become habituated and require less and less conscious effort to execute them.

Principle #2: Improvisation Is Natural
Improvisation is a natural part of the human experience. In new situations, humans draw upon past memories (learned experiences) to resolve conflict and, when needed, imagine new solutions. Human imagination has been the catalyst for progress in every aspect of civilization: government, science, medicine, business, industry, and art.

Principle #3: Improvisation = Memory + Imagination
Improvisation is a skill and, like all skills, can be acquired (learned) and refined (improved) with practice.

Principle #4: Musical Improvisation = Musical Memories + Musical imagination
Musical improvisation is the combination of musical memories and musical imagination.

Principle #5: Three Types of Musical Memories—Aural, Intellectual, Kinesthetic
There are three types of musical memories: **aural** (what we hear in our mind's ear), **intellectual** (what we see in our mind's eye), and **kinesthetic** (what we feel in our body). The most powerful musical memory is aural (the sound of music). The most powerful memory for the jazz improviser is the sound of jazz in their mind's

ear. The more we have heard and internalized jazz, the better we can imagine new jazz sounds that reflect our unique musical personality.

Principle #6: Listening Is Fundamental and the Best First Step

Principle #7: Melody = The Most Indelible Musical Memory
The basic elements of music are **melody**, **harmony**, and **rhythm**. Of those, melody is the most memorable because a well-crafted melody can imply both harmony and rhythm. The greatest jazz improvisations do that. For the student, listening and imitating great solos is fundamental to the process.

Principle #8: There Is No "One Way" to Learn Jazz and No "One Way" to Run the Changes
There are a variety of ways to learn jazz and how to run the changes. They often intersect and overlap to some degree, but they are by and large unique. Some require an intellectual approach to theory while others require a more intuitive approach.

Principle #9: Improvisation Is Best When It's Less about Thinking and More about "Hearing" Something New in the Mind's Ear
Jazz musicians are often asked: "What are you thinking about when improvising?" The best answer might be another question: "What were you thinking when you asked that?" Our thoughts lead to spoken language and our musical thoughts lead to musical language. A thought is more than just a word, phrase, or sentence. A musical thought is more than just a note or notes, or a phrase, etc. The goal of the jazz musician is to express a musical thought, hopefully one that is (or seems to be) unique or novel in the moment. *Running the Changes* is designed to help students at all levels, from beginning to advanced, have better access to the musical thoughts that best express their musical personality. Eventually, those will become one's personal sound.

Principle #10: Improvisation = Play
This book is grounded in the philosophy that improvisation is a natural part of human behavior and blossoms organically through imitation and exploration (Principle #2). These activities in children are characterized as "play." The best creative endeavors of adults have the same "play-like" quality. That quality is the thing that attracts some us to jazz and jazz improvisation. Those who have made jazz performance their profession are not only invited to play music but, more importantly, to "play with" music. Well-informed jazz listeners, when presented with creatively inspired improvisations, are able to enjoy that sense of "play" as well.

Principle #11: Improvisation Should Be Fun
Although the process may seem arduous at times (more like work than play), students are advised to remain positive. Each mistake is a lesson in what not to do. The more mistakes we make in our practice, the more we are learning in a way. Have fun! Enjoy your mistakes!

Principle #12: Successful Jazz Improvisation Involves Many Different Skills
Jazz improvisation is best understood as not just one skill but a set of skills acquired through practice and accessed by a performer in real time. It may seem that these skills are retrieved simultaneously in the improviser's mind, but science suggests it is more likely they are being executed in a sequence of neural activities that may last only a fraction of a second. Quick access is the key—that is why repetitive practice is so important.

How To Use This Book

Running the Changes is organized into three levels that present detailed descriptions of 12 discrete (individual) skills important in creating jazz improvisations in the bebop tradition. Each of those chapters include a demonstration solo/etude. Some chapters are theory lessons that provide information needed to understand material that follows. Students with a solid theoretical foundation may opt to skip over those chapters or skim them briefly. The Appendix includes an essay on post-bop approaches to harmony and practice progressions for the audio tracks.

 To access the audio tracks, go to *www.halleonard.com/mylibrary* and input the code found on page 1.

Level One

Level One of *Running the Changes* presents three techniques that are part of nearly every jazz solo.

Melodic Paraphrase, Using Riffs, and Quoting Common Jazz Phrases

These concepts are not complicated, and when executed with expertise, they can produce beautiful jazz solos. To a large degree, they are intuitive and may come naturally to some, particularly those that have had generous prior exposure to jazz. It has been my experience that some students struggle with these basic steps and need to spend a bit more time solidifying these fundamental skills before proceeding to more advanced topics. It has also been my experience that teachers, like myself, for whom these basic skills came easily, may tend to overlook their importance. A key component in being able to use melodic paraphrase, riffs, and quotes will be the improviser's command of rhythmic elements. Rhythm is the most important element in jazz performance.

It's Gotta Dance

It has been said that: "Music is only about one of two things—song or dance." If that statement is true, then jazz is mostly about "dance." The rhythm of jazz is firmly rooted in the musics of Africa and the Carribean, both of which contain a strong connection to physical movement. Even though we no longer think of jazz as being primarily for dancing, rhythm and rhythmic movement remain a core element.

Dance Versus March

How do we define dance or, more specifically, music for dancing? In general, dance music has a rhythmic pulse and is related to a meter much like march music. We march to a rhythmic pulse, which is in meter, but a marching person is seldom mistaken for a dancing person. Dancing has more variety of movement and a looser interpretation of the pulse than marching. Many times, a dance step will play against the pulse and meter. For example, the basic fox-trot step (and jitterbug step as well) is organized in three (3/4) while the meter of the music is in four (4/4). Jazz rhythm must not only agree with the pulse; it should also *play* with the pulse.

Swing—Accuracy and Interpretation

Swing is a great word, but it can be misunderstood to mean a particular style or particular rhythmic subdivision (i.e., a triplet feel). In a general sense, swing is a combination of rhythmic accuracy (agreeing with a pulse) and a characteristic interpretation of the beat. Interpretation of the beat might be a simple as accenting beats 2 and 4 in 4/4 time or accenting upbeat eighth notes in a bop style. The best path to achieving a great rhythmic feel is through directed listening and emulation. More casually put, I would say: Play along with recordings—a lot. Jazz needs to *swing*.

Developing Rhythm Awareness by Listening and Playing Along with Recordings

The following steps may leave you feeling that you've "jumped into the deep end and you can't swim." Stick with it and "keep paddling," eventually, you will be swimming effortlessly. This is terrific training and can benefit every improviser, regardless of their level.

1. Pick a recording you like—just one song.
2. Listen carefully to the entire track.
3. Listen again focusing on the drums and bass. Play/sing along on one pitch.
4. Listen to the solos and play along, trying to copy the rhythms on one pitch.
5. Improvise your own rhythms (on one pitch) that compliment (fit with) the solos.
6. With attention to rhythm, experiment with other pitches.
7. Repeat the process with the same song or choose another.

Chapter 1: Using Melodic Paraphrase

Listen First

- **Frank Sinatra** – "Fly Me to the Moon" (*It Might as Well Be Spring*, Decca 1964)

- **Ella Fitzgerald** – "How High the Moon" (*Ella in Berlin*, Verve 1960)

- **Louis Armstrong** – "Mack the Knife" (*Satchmo the Great*, 1956)

- **Frank Sinatra** – "Somebody Loves Me" (*Sinatra Sings Gershwin*, Columbia 2003)

With very few exceptions, jazz performances usually begin and end with a statement of the melody of a song. Improvisers often incorporate parts of the melody into solos or create slightly different versions of the melody by **paraphrasing** (reinventing or personalizing parts of the basic melody). Melodic paraphrase and riff playing, the main devices of jazz soloing in the Swing era, are often overlooked by beginners or teachers working with beginners. Learning melodies and riffs is crucial in the development of improvisational skill.

Two Distinct Skills: Melodic Reinvention and Melodic Ornamentation

Definitions

- **Melodic Reinvention:** Altering a melody by changing its rhythms without adding new pitches.

- **Melodic Ornamentation:** Altering a melody by adding new pitches.

Melodic reinvention and melodic ornamentation are quite distinct. Successful reinvention only requires musical imagination and a good feel for jazz rhythm. It grows "organically" (naturally) from the imagined melodies in the "mind's ear" of the performer. Successful ornamentation is more advance than reinvention and usually requires at least a basic knowledge of keys, scales, chords and jazz vocabulary. (We will learn about it in Level Two.)

Rhythm is the jazz improviser's most powerful tool and the central element of jazz style. Early ragtime and jazz musicians used rhythmic devices to reinvent the melodies that they heard around them: field hollers, gospel songs, blues, minstrel songs, marches, classical music, etc. They called it "raggin' the melody" (after ragtime). *All melodic reinvention in jazz is rhythmic.* There are seven ways we rhythmically reinvent a melody: 1) Syncopation; 2) Iteration; 3) Displacement; 4) Augmentation; 5) Diminution; 6) Repetition; and 7) Truncation.

1. **Syncopation**—"Play Some Notes Early and Some Notes Late"

2. **Iteration**—"Fill It Up with Rhythm"

3. **Displacement**—"Move It Around"

4. **Augmentation**—"Stretch It Out"

5. **Diminution**—"Push It Together"

6. **Repetition**—"Go Back and Play It Again"

7. **Truncation**—"Leave Some of It Out"

Play through the following reinvented version of "Somebody Loves Me" and observe how melodic reinvention adds rhythmic interest and "jazziness." On the repeat, make up your own reinventions.

Somebody Loves Me

Using Melodic Paraphrase (Reinvention)

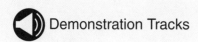 Demonstration Tracks

To access the material indicated by the icon above, just head over to **www.halleonard.com/mylibrary** *and input the code found on page 1 of this book!*

Track 1 (Trumpet)

Track 2 (Tenor Saxophone)

Track 3 (Trombone)

Track 4 (Vocal)

Track 5 (Rhythm Track)

SOMEBODY LOVES ME
Using Melodic Paraphrase (Reinvention)

C Treble Clef Instruments

Music by George Gershwin
Lyrics by Ballard MacDonald
and Buddy DeSylva

Somebody Loves Me
Using Melodic Paraphrase (Reinvention)

Bb Instruments

Music by George Gershwin
Lyrics by Ballard MacDonald
and Buddy DeSylva

Somebody Loves Me
Using Melodic Paraphrase (Reinvention)

Eb Instruments

Music by George Gershwin
Lyrics by Ballard MacDonald
and Buddy DeSylva

Somebody Loves Me
Using Melodic Paraphrase (Reinvention)

C Vocal Instruments

Music by George Gershwin
Lyrics by Ballard MacDonald
and Buddy DeSylva

Somebody Loves Me
Using Melodic Paraphrase (Reinvention)

C Bass Clef Instruments

Music by George Gershwin
Lyrics by Ballard MacDonald
and Buddy DeSylva

How to Practice Melodic Paraphrase

- Step 1: Make a list of all the melodies you can sing and/or play on your instrument with accuracy (pitches and rhythms). This is what you are actually hearing in your "mind's ear," and it will make up your basic melodic vocabulary.

- Step 2: Using the melodies on your list, experiment with different ways of playing and/or singing them while keeping them recognizable.

- Step 3: Make a list of jazz tunes you want to learn. Memorize the melody for each tune, and then take each phrase and play them differently. Experiment.

- Step 4: Listen to your favorite improvisers and notice how they reinvent melodies. Pay particular attention to jazz singers. They may be the most help in demonstrating how melodies can be reinvented.

Important Things to Remember

- Keep what works and discard (or avoid in the future) what doesn't work.

- Learning to improvise is just as much a process of discovering what doesn't work, as it is a process of discovering what does work.

Chapter 2: Using Riffs

Listen First

- **Paul Williams** – "The Hucklebuck" (Savoy 1949)

- **Jimmy Forrest** – "Night Train" (*Night Train*, Delmark 1953)

- **Lambert Hendricks and Ross** – "Centerpiece" (*The Hottest New Group in Jazz*, Columbia 1959)

- **Louis Jordan** – "Choo Choo Ch'Boogie" (*Best of Louis Jordan*, Decca 1946)

- **Dexter Gordon** – "Apple Jump" (*Biting the Apple*, Inner City 1976)

Definitions

- **Riffs:** Short melodic fragments of common clichéd jazz vocabulary.

- **Blues Riffs:** Short melodic fragments that have a blues feeling by emphasizing blue notes.

- **Blue Notes:** Often the flatted 3rd, 5th, and 7th of a key.

- **Cliché:** A phrase or expression that is common to a genre.

Jazz soloists, since the earliest years of the art form, have used common clichéd short phrases called riffs in their improvisations. Clichés can, if overused, make a solo predictable and uninteresting; however, if used with taste and rhythmic vitality, they can add authenticity to a solo. Riffs with distinctive blues feeling were a large part of the improvisational vocabulary of the Swing era (circa 1930 to 1940). Many of the song melodies of that era, plus blues songs throughout the history of jazz, are made up of blues riffs.

Use this list of riff-oriented melodies to acquaint your ears to blues riffs. These song melodies are simple enough that you can learn them in one or two listenings. Play and sing along with them.

- "Bags' Groove"
- "Splanky"
- "Sonnymoon for Two"
- "Blues Walk"
- "Lester Leaps In"
- "Short Stop"
- "Night Train"
- "Birk's Works"
- "Blues in the Closet"
- "Jumpin' with Symphony Sid"
- "Blue Monk"
- "Buzzy"
- "Cold Duck Time"

- "Cool Blues"
- "St. Louis Blues"
- "Bunny Hop"
- "Tenor Madness"
- "Blues for Duane"
- "The Hucklebuck"
- "Section Blues"
- "Bags 'n Trane"
- "Things Ain't What They Used to Be"
- "Duke's Place"
- "Blues by Five"
- "Centerpiece"
- "Bessie's Blues"

While these riffs can sound jazzy and fit well with the blues progression, they don't necessarily work well as change-running devices in non-blues progressions. With clever use, they can be made to sound well at the ends of phrases where the changes are static. Remember, in a way, these are "spice," and too much spice can "spoil the meal."

Riffs are usually oriented to a key and may tend to stress the tonic (key note). Often, musically successful riffs can be created using only the tonic note, played with emphatic rhythm. Most riffs use some blues expression, such as bending notes or scooping into notes. The use of "blue notes," or notes that are dissonant to the key of the song, is a common device as well.

Blue Notes

C Major Scale

C Major Scale with Blue Notes

Blues Scales

Many may find it helpful to organize riff vocabulary into scale forms, which are called **blues scales**. This has some benefit, but it is important to remember that there is more than one form of the blues scale. Here are the three most common blues scale constructions.

C Minor Blues Scale

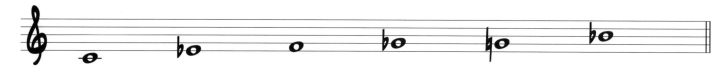

C Major Blues Scale

C Composite Blues Scale

Getting the Blues Feeling Using Common Jazz Expressions

Jazz musicians often manipulate the pitch of certain notes (primarily blue notes) to add a bluesy feeling to their solos. There are many different ways to achieve these effects, and the techniques will vary from instrument to instrument. Listen carefully to blues oriented players to get the sound of these expressions in your mind's ear, and attempt to imitate them first by singing them. After you can approximate the sounds with your voice, try them on your instrument. Here are the most common jazz expressions.

Bend
Start on the pitch and bend it down.

Doit
Slide the pitch upward at the end of the note.

Scoop
Slide into the pitch from below.

Plop
Slide down to the pitch from the note above.

Fall
Let the pitch fall at the end of the note.

Glissando
Slide from one note to the next smoothly.

Flip
Also called a **turn**, the flip is executed by quickly playing a note above the original, returning to the original note, and then proceeding to the next note.

Finding the Roots of Riffs in Rhythm 'n' Blues

In the late 1940s and into the 1950s, a sub-genre of jazz called **rhythm 'n' blues** became extremely popular. It grew out of "jump" music from the Swing era in reaction to the complexity of bebop and, in many ways, was the predecessor of early rock 'n' roll. The song melodies in "R&B" and the solo material of the style were almost exclusively created using riffs. The R&B genre enjoyed widespread popularity. Most professional dance musicians in that era and, into the 1960s, learned to emulate the vocabulary and style out of sheer economic necessity. The greatest jazz musicians of the time, such as Charlie Parker, Cannonball Adderley, Miles Davis, and others, would include similar riffs in their solos. Young musicians who are unfamiliar with the style would do well to study it. The following chart provides some classic recordings from the era.

Riffs can be very short, yet quite effective in jazz solos. Here is a list of very common two-note, three-note, and four-note blues riffs in the key of C.

Typical Two-Note Riffs in the Key of C

Typical Three-Note Riffs in the Key of C

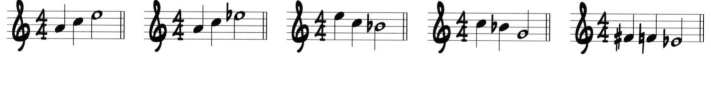

Typical Four-Note Riffs in the Key of C

Don't let the simplicity of these riffs fool you. When they are applied with rhythmic imagination and creative reinvention (as we discussed in Chapter 1), they can create effective and characteristic jazz solos. The next etude ("Keepin' It Simple Blues") is composed using only basic two- and three-note riffs.

Note: While many of the articulations written in the chart highlight typical jazz expressions within a phrase, the players on the demonstration tracks may deviate from what's written, showing the degree of individualization jazz musicians take when playing melodies with a rhythm section accompanying them.

Keepin' It Simple Blues

Using Two- and Three-Note Riffs and Melodic Reinvention

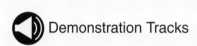 Demonstration Tracks

Track 6 (Trumpet)

Track 7 (Alto Saxophone)

Track 8 (Guitar)

Track 9 (Vocal)

Track 10 (Rhythm Track)

Keepin' It Simple Blues

Using Two- and Three-Note Riffs and Melodic Reinvention

C Treble Clef Instruments

Mike Steinel

Keepin' It Simple Blues

Using Two- and Three-Note Riffs and Melodic Reinvention

Bb Instruments

Mike Steinel

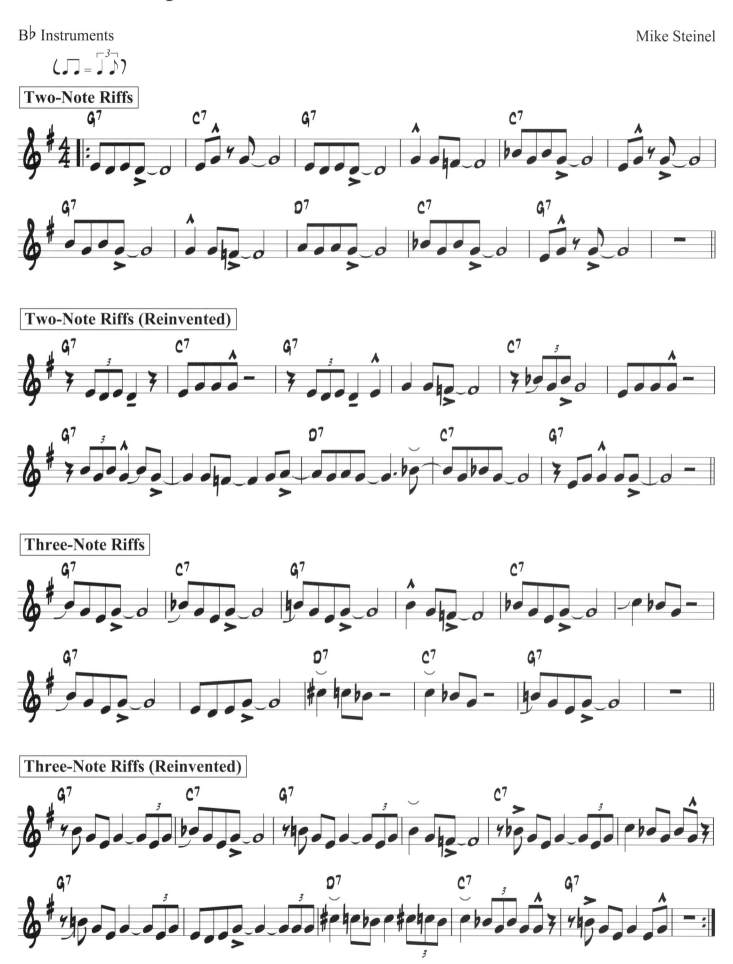

27

Keepin' It Simple Blues

Using Two- and Three-Note Riffs and Melodic Reinvention

E♭ Instruments

Mike Steinel

KEEPIN' IT SIMPLE BLUES
Using Two- and Three-Note Riffs and Melodic Reinvention

C Bass Clef Instruments

Mike Steinel

Riffs can be longer. Here are common one- and two-bar riffs.

Common One-Bar Riffs in C Major

Common Two-Bar Riffs in C Major

"Blues for Buddy" (on the next page) demonstrates how simple riffs played with characteristic jazz expression can be used to build effective solos.

Blues for Buddy

Using Riffs

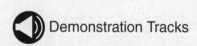 Demonstration Tracks

Track 11 (Trumpet)

Track 12 (Alto Saxophone)

Track 13 (Trombone)

Track 14 (Vocal)

Track 15 (Rhythm Track)

Blues for Buddy
Using Riffs

C Treble Clef Instruments

Mike Steinel

Blues for Buddy

Using Riffs

Bb Instruments

Mike Steinel

Blues for Buddy

Using Riffs

Eb Instruments

Mike Steinel

Blues for Buddy

Using Riffs

C Bass Clef Instruments

Mike Steinel

Chapter 3: Quoting Jazz Phrases

The development of a personalized jazz vocabulary is similar to the process humans experience when learning a spoken language. Infants begin by imitating the sounds around them, and about age one, they start using simple words. As they interact with parents and older siblings, they begin to speak in phrases (groups of words). Students learning a foreign language start with single words but quickly move to key phrases such as "thank you," "good evening," etc. They learn to converse (hold a conversation) not by inventing their own phrases but by using phrases everyone will understand. Most jazz musicians, even the most advanced, have gone through the same process in learning a jazz vocabulary.

Remember from the Introduction: *All human learning is imitation and exploration.* Imitation comes first. Chapter 1 introduced melodic paraphrase. Chapter 2 introduced riffs and blues expressions. This chapter will introduce common one- and two-bar phrases that students can absorb quickly to make their solos more conversational. The process is simple: Learn these phrases from all 12 starting notes until you can play them accurately from memory at a medium tempo. Trust your intuition (your musical ear) to help you find when and where these phrases can be best used in your solos.

You Are Part of a Tradition

The tradition of imitation is a common thread in jazz history.

> Bird imitated Lester Young, Trane imitated Bird, Roy Eldridge imitated Coleman Hawkins, Dizzy Gillespie imitated Roy Eldridge, and on and on.

Chords, scales, and modes are the "alphabet" of jazz. Common phrases are the "sentences" of jazz. The trick is to remember that **phrase quoting** is only a preliminary step. To make a mature and personal statement in jazz performance, improvisers must go beyond this first step and learn to "break down" the language, understand the grammar of jazz line, and get to the "word level" of this music. Failing that, their solos will sound stiff, predictable, and banal. (We will begin that process in Level Two.)

Practice the phrases on the next page to get them in your ear, voice, and fingers, and then transpose each phrase to all 12 notes of the chromatic scale. Study transcriptions by your favorite performers, find your own favorite phrases, and record them in a notebook. Remember: This is an intermediate step, and solos created by assembling these phrases may sound academic or stiff. Many of these phrases will return later in this book, as we study the theory to understand why they work and how they are related to particular chords or groups of chords. For practice, sing and play them from all 12 notes and experiment using them in your solos.

Common One-Bar Jazz Phrases

Common Two-Bar Jazz Phrases

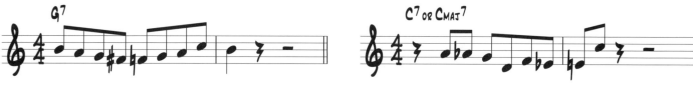

Three Phrases from Early Pop/Jazz Tunes

Opening Phrase of "Fascinating Rhythm" (George Gershwin, 1924)

Opening Phrase of "Sweet Georgia Brown" (Maceo Pinkard, 1925)

Opening Phrase of "I Love a Piano" (Irving Berlin, 1915)

Each of the songs listed on this page has a distinctive melody and rhythm that can be easily quoted in jazz soloing. Some come from earlier periods of jazz performance, and you may not be familiar with them. They will be familiar to an informed jazz audience. Use what appeals to you. Often, the opening phrase of the tune will provide the most effective material. Add new tunes as you discover them.

Tunes From Early Jazz and the Swing Era

- "12th Street Rag"
- "When the Saints Go Marching In"
- "Back Home in Indiana"
- "Sweet Georgia Brown"
- "Alexander's Ragtime Band"
- "Way Down Yonder in New Orleans"
- "Do You Know the Way to New Orleans?"
- "Basin Street Blues"

- "St. Louis Blues"
- "Opus One"
- "Oh Lady Be Good"
- "Crazy Rhythm"
- "Fascinating Rhythm"
- "Night Train"
- "In the Mood"
- "Chattanooga Choo Choo"

Tunes by or Associated with Duke Ellington and Billy Strayhorn

- "Don't Get Around Much Anymore"
- "Satin Doll"
- "Take the 'A' Train"
- "It Don't Mean a Thing If It Ain't Got That Swing"

- "Cottontail"
- "Perdido"
- "In a Mellow Tone"
- "I Got It Bad and That Ain't Good"

Bebop Tunes by Charlie Parker, Dizzy Gillespie, or Thelonious Monk

- "Groovin' High" (Dizzy)
- "Birk's Works" (Dizzy)
- "A Night in Tunisia" (Dizzy)
- "Salt Peanuts" (Dizzy)
- "Woody n' You" (Dizzy)
- "Ornithology" (Parker)
- "Yardbird Suite" (Parker)
- "Anthropology" (Parker)
- "Confirmation" (Parker)

- "Scrapple from the Apple" (Parker)
- "Billie's Bounce" (Parker)
- "My Little Suede Shoes" (Parker)
- "Well You Needn't" (Monk)
- "'Round Midnight" (Monk)
- "Blue Monk" (Monk)
- "Bemsha Swing" (Monk)
- "52nd Street Theme" (Monk)
- "In Walked Bud" (Monk)

Other Jazz Tunes and Distinctive Pop Tunes

- "Four" (Miles Davis)
- "Solar" (Miles Davis)
- "The Theme" (Miles Davis)
- "Dig" (Miles Davis)
- "Doxy" (Sonny Rollins)
- "Oleo" (Sonny Rollins)
- "Pent Up House" (Sonny Rollins)
- "St. Thomas" (Sonny Rollins)

- "Impressions" (John Coltrane)
- "Moment's Notice" (John Coltrane)
- "Mr. PC" (John Coltrane)
- "Footprints" (Wayne Shorter)
- "Witch Hunt" (Wayne Shorter)
- "Recordame" (Joe Henderson)
- "Blue Bossa" (Kenny Dorham)
- "Mercy, Mercy, Mercy" (Joe Zawinul)

Play the etude on the next page to get a feel for how a solo can be constructed by quoting typical jazz phrases. If it sounds "dry" and not very jazzy, try applying the concepts of melodic paraphrase (Chapter 1) and jazz expression (Chapter 2) for a more personalized sound. Experiment and explore!

Some Stray Horns

Quoting Common Jazz Melodies

 Demonstration Tracks

Track 16 (Trumpet)

Track 17 (Alto Saxophone)

Track 18 (Trombone)

Track 19 (Guitar)

Track 20 (Vocal)

Track 21 (Rhythm Track)

SOME STRAY HORNS
Quoting Common Jazz Melodies

C Treble Clef Instruments

Mike Steinel

SOME STRAY HORNS
Quoting Common Jazz Melodies

Bb Instruments

Mike Steinel

Some Stray Horns
Quoting Common Jazz Melodies

E♭ Instruments

Mike Steinel

Some Stray Horns
Quoting Common Jazz Melodies

C Bass Clef Instruments

Mike Steinel

Level Two

Level One of *Running the Changes* introduced students to three foundational improvisation skills: 1) using melodic paraphrase; 2) using riffs; and 3) quoting common jazz phrases. Effective use of those techniques in jazz soloing requires little or no intellectual understanding of jazz harmony or what is often called **chord/scale theory**. Using only devices from Level One, performers with strong aural skills, an equally strong feeling for jazz rhythm, and a creative imagination can produce solos of a high artistic level. Certainly, some of the most famous improvisers in jazz history achieved their great artistry with little or no study of harmony. However, we should not let that fact stop us from continuing our study of change running.

The material in Level Two will require at least a fundamental understanding of jazz harmony. Chapter 4 covers the basics of chord construction and chord nomenclature (labeling). Chapter 8 introduces basic scale and mode theory. If you have a solid understanding of these topics, you may wish to skip these lessons or review them briefly. Of prime importance going forward will be the command of: 1) modes of the major scale; 2) modes of harmonic minor; 3) modes of harmonic major; 4) diminished scales; and 5) whole tone scales. The preliminary exercises included in Level Two should become part of your daily practice.

The order of the chapters in Level Two may seem odd. I have purposely introduced chord tone soloing (Chapter 6) and ornamentation of color tones (Chapter 7) before introducing scales and mode soloing. Many jazz educators start with the chord/scale approach, but I have found that doing so often leads to soloing that lacks harmonic strength and accuracy. The chord/scale approach became popular in the late '50s and into the '60s due to the modal music in vogue during that period. What is often overlooked is the fact that musicians such as Miles Davis and John Coltrane, who championed the modal approach, had grown up learning change running techniques in the Bebop era and were masters at change running before they experimented with approaches that focused more on scales. Not every tone of the scale carries equal weight, and most students arrive at a more mature approach to scale/mode soloing if they first develop a sensitivity to chord tones in general and color tone ornamentation in particular. The harmonic strength of melody in jazz is generated mainly with chord tones. Starting with scales puts the "cart before the horse," in a way.

Level Two Outline

Chapter 4: Basic Chord Theory

Chapter 5: Basic Ornamentation

Chapter 6: Chord Tone Soloing

Chapter 7: Ornamenting the Melody of the 3rd

Chapter 8: Basic Scale/Mode Theory

Chapter 9: Scale/Mode Soloing

Chapter 4: Basic Chord Theory

Chords in jazz can be as small as three notes (triads) and as large as seven notes (13th chords). They are constructed by stacking every other note of a scale. Chord tones get their names (labels) from the distance in steps they are from the tonic note (root) of the chord.

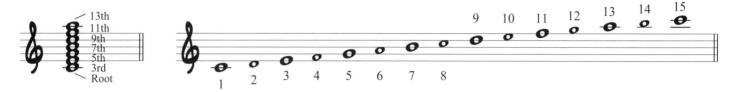

At the most basic level, all jazz chords are one of three basic types: major, dominant, and minor. Elevenths of major and dominant chords are dissonant and, in general practice, left out (in improvisations and chord accompaniments) or raised one half step. These raised notes are called **sharp 11ths** (#11) and are common in jazz harmony. Here are the three basic 13th-chord types in modern jazz.

Chord knowledge is useless without an understanding of how chords are labeled and interpreted by jazz musicians. Although there is some variation, for the most part it works like this:

Letters or symbols after the root indicate the quality for minors and majors

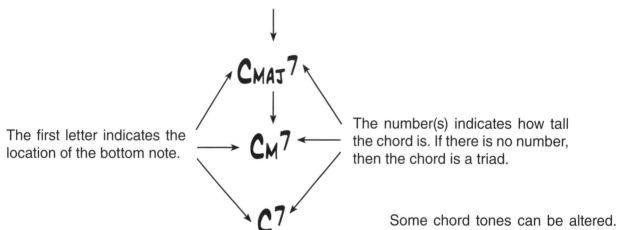

The first letter indicates the location of the bottom note.

The number(s) indicates how tall the chord is. If there is no number, then the chord is a triad.

If the chord is dominant, there will be nothing between the root and the number.

Some chord tones can be altered. Those alterations are indicated with a sharp or flat sign (# or ♭).

There are variations in labeling the quality of chords:

- Cmaj7: CM7, CMaj7, CMa7, or Cmaj

- Cm7: Cmin7, Cmi7, C-7

- C7: C7

The Major Chord Family

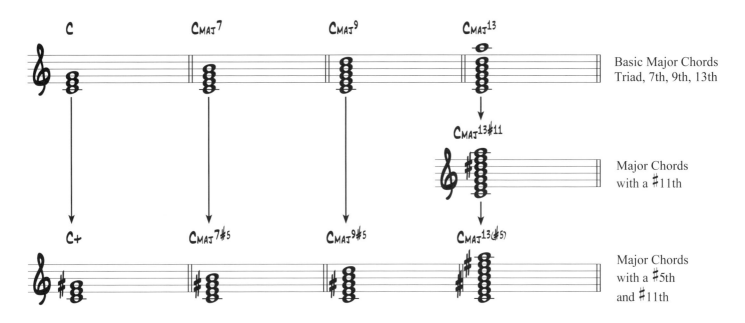

Basic Major Chords
Triad, 7th, 9th, 13th

Major Chords
with a ♯11th

Major Chords
with a ♯5th
and ♯11th

The Minor Chord Family

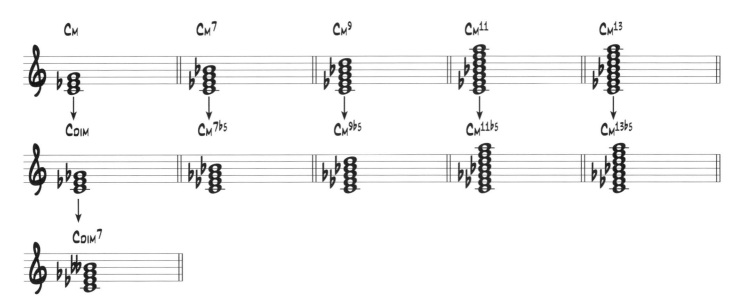

The Dominant Chord Family

The dominant chord in jazz performance usually contains at least one upper extension (9th, 11th, ♯11th, or 13th). As mentioned earlier, the natural 11th is dissonant with the 3rd of the chord, so it is either raised (♯11th) or it used when the 3rd is omitted. Here are the basic dominant chords:

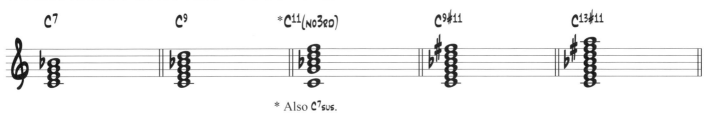

* Also C7sus.

The dominant chord is the most pliable of the three basic chord types, and if the root, 3rd, and 7th remain the same, the other tones (5th, 9th, 11th, and 13th) may be altered. Tones like 5ths and 9ths may be raised or lowered, while the 11th may be raised and the 13th may be lowered. Basically, the altered dominant chords can be organized into four types:

- Dominants with altered 5ths (raised or lowered)

- Dominants with altered 9ths (raised or lowered)

- Dominants with lowered 13ths and altered 9ths (raised or lowered)

- Dominants with altered 5ths and 9ths (raised or lowered)

Dominants with Altered 5ths

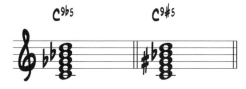

Dominants with Altered 9ths

Dominants with Altered 9ths and 13ths

Dominants with Altered 9ths and 5ths

Common Use of Chord Extensions and Alterations

The use of extensions and alterations in jazz performance will vary to some degree, depending on the style of the music and the level of musicianship of the pianist or guitarist in the group. However, these guidelines usually apply: It is assumed in modern jazz that all chord voicings contain some extension such as a 9th, 11th, or 13th, even if the symbols on the lead sheet indicate 7th chords. If the chords are listed as 13ths, 11ths, or 9ths, it is not a given that all the chord tones will be present in the accompaniment. As a matter of fact, voicings that contain all the chord tones usually sound too "thick" to be effective.

Preliminary Chord Exercises

Practice these three exercises until you can play them without error and from memory at a moderate tempo (♪ = 144 BPM) from all 12 notes. If you need to write them out, do so.

Exercise 1

Continue practicing this exercise, moving through all 12 keys.

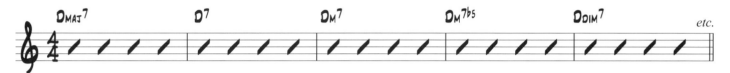

Exercise 2

Continue practicing this exercise, moving through all 12 keys.

Exercise 3

Continue practicing this exercise, moving through all 12 keys.

If you want more ideas on how to practice chords, you may find my book *Building a Jazz Vocabulary* (Hal Leonard) to be helpful.

Chapter 5: Basic Ornamentation

Definitions

- **Musical Ornamentation:** Extra notes added to a melody to make it more elaborate.

- **Target Notes:** Important melody notes to which ornaments are applied.

- **Lower Neighbor Tones:** Notes that move down a step and then return to a target note.

- **Upper Neighbor Tones:** Notes that move up a step and then return to a target note.

- **Enclosure:** Two notes that approach a target from above and below.

- **Passing Tones:** Notes added between chord tones or scale tones.

- **Approach Tones:** Notes added in front of target notes.

- **Departure Tones:** Notes added after target notes.

The embellishments in this chapter, which are called ornaments, are like the jazz expressions (bends, glissandi, and falls) introduced in the chapter on riffs. However, jazz ornamentation is more elaborate and can add extra pitches to basic melodies. Some ornaments can be as short as one note or as long as three or four.

Ornamenting Target Tones

Approach Tones from Above and Below

Departure Tones

Combining Approach Tones, Departure Tones, and Passing Tones

Approach Tone Ornamentation of Target Notes

Any note can be "targeted" but in most jazz improvisation, targets notes are those with harmonic strength or melodic importance. Ornaments that lead into target notes (approach tones) and resolve convincingly can produce interesting jazz melodies. Approach notes needn't fit the underlying harmony as long as they resolve with strength into the target note. The strongest resolutions are "by step" from above or below. The chart below illustrates various combinations.

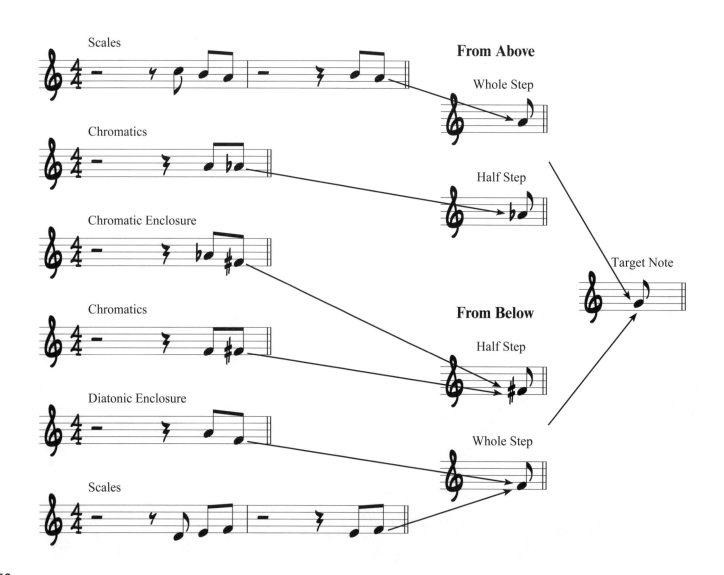

Approach tones resolve well into 3rds of chords.

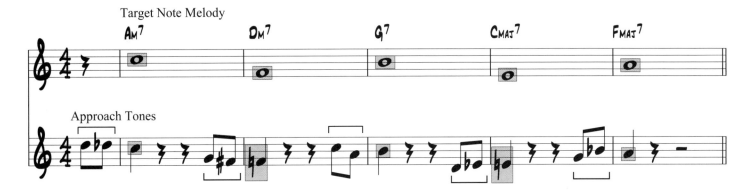

Basic Departure Note Ornamentation of Target Tones

After target notes, other tones can be added using steps or leaps (scales or chords) in ascending (up in pitch) or descending (down in pitch) motion.

Departure tones after target notes should agree harmonically with the underlying chord and key center.

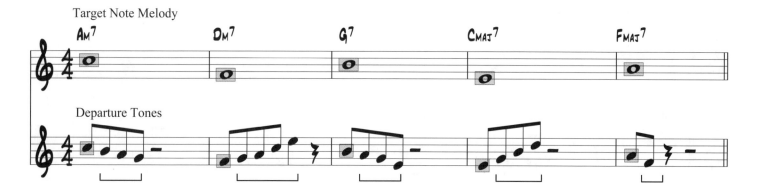

Connecting Approach Tones and Departure Tones

Jazz melodies are often composed of long passages of eighth notes. In order to maintain eighth-note motion, the improviser must be able to connect departure tones from one target note to the approach tones of the next target. If the approach tones and departure tones are ingrained through repetition, then the improviser's chord/scale knowledge, technical command of scales, and basic harmonic intuition will aid them in chosing notes that connect smoothly.

Chapter 6: Chord Tone Soloing

Definitions

- **Color Tones:** Tones that determine the quality of the chord (the 3rd and 7th are the most common color tones).

- **Extensions/Tension Tones:** the 9th, 11th, and 13th.

- **Altered Tones:** lowered or raised 5ths, 9ths, 11ths, and 13ths.

The principles of **chord tone soloing** are drawn from basic, centuries-old compositional practices. In Chapter 4, we learned that jazz chords have as many as seven tones (root, 3rd, 5th, 7th, 9th, 11th, and 13th), but not all tones are of equal harmonic strength. The 3rd and 7th do the most to determine the basic quality of the chord (major, minor, dominant, etc.). The root determines location while the 5th is passive and is often omitted in the accompaniment. The 9th, 11th, and 13th are considered "tension notes" and usually need to be resolved to a lower chord tone such as the root, 3rd, or 5th. When 5ths, 9ths, 11ths, and 13ths are altered they may be treated as color tones.

- **13th:** Tension note (should resolve)

- **11th:** Tension note (should resolve)

- **9th:** Tension note (useable as a color tone)

- **7th:** Color tone (determines quality)

- **5th:** Not a color tone (unless altered)

- **3rd:** Color tone (determines quality)

- **Root:** Determines location (cannot be altered)

Guidelines for Chord Tone Soloing

1. Whenever possible, put chord tones on downbeats.

2. Avoid skipping between non-chord tones (including the 11th and 13th).

3. At the point of chord change, always connect by step or from chord tone to chord tone.

4. Stressed non-chord tones should resolve into chord tones (1, 3, 5, and 7).

5. Include the 3rd to ensure complete suggestion of the chord.

6. Omit the root (or avoid stressing it) to avoid "heaviness."

7. Use eighth-note motion predominantly.

8. Add triplets for rhythmic interest (common on beats 2 and 4).

The music of the Bebop era provides excellent examples of chord tone soloing, but it is often obscured by the use of chromatic ornamentation (discussed in the next chapter). It may be helpful to study the solos of pre-bop players such as Lester Young, Coleman Hawkins, and Benny Goodman for more obvious examples of chord tone soloing. Bebop players such as Charlie Parker learned to play by copying Swing era players such as Young, Hawkins, and Goodman and borrowed heavily from their material which included melodic paraphrase, riffs, and chord tone melodies. Here are three great pre-bop solos that display great chord tone soloing.

Artist	Song	Recording Date
Lester Young	"The Man I Love"	1937
Colman Hawkins	"Body and Soul"	1939
Benny Goodman	"Seven Come Eleven"	1939

Getting Started—Chord Tone Soloing

At first glance, it might seem that the variations of chord tones would be almost infinite. In fact, we can organize chord tone melodies used in jazz into a small set of basic forms, practice those over the various harmonies of our repertoire, then use our musical imaginations to invent variations which fit our musical needs.

The basic forms of chord tone soloing, applied to 7th and 9th chords, as used by pre-bop and bebop musicians are:

1. Ascending arpeggio (most common)

2. Descending arpeggio (common, but not as common as ascending arpeggios)

3. Ascending inversion (used sparingly)

4. Descending inversion (common)

5. Scrambled forms (somewhat rare)

Basic Chord Tone Forms

Ascending Arpeggios

Descending Arpeggios

Ascending Inversions

Descending Inversions

Scrambled Forms

Making Chord Tone Soloing Interesting

Students may avoid using chord tone soloing because it seems too obvious and boring. That would be the case if we do little more than the simple arpeggiation of chords from their roots. Play or sing the first line of the excerpt below. Although it is a very complete suggestion of the changes, it falls short in sounding interesting or jazzy. The second line, which begins with descending motion from the 9th, is better but still a bit obvious.

Seven Principles to Create Interest

Principle #1: Avoid beginning arpeggios on the root of the chord. Try starting arpeggios on the 3rd or 5th of the chord (3-5-7-9, 5-7-9-1-1). Resolve arpeggios into strong tones like the root, 3rd, or 5th for best results.

Principle #2: Use the common descending form of 5-3-1-7, also starting on the 9th (9-7-5-4 resolving to the 3rd).

Principle #3: Add chromatic approach tones (single or double) before any chord form.

Principle #4 and #5: Avoid starting on the downbeat and use triplets to add rhythmic variety (commonly on beat 2).

Principle #6: Add passing diatonic notes between any chord tones, except where it might put an 11th or 13th on a downbeat or a skip between a tension note (4 or 6).

These sound like Cmaj7:

These do not sound like Cmaj7:

By adding passing tones to chord tones, smooth (almost scale-like) melodies can be created. If the rule of avoiding skips is applied between non-chord tones, the melody will imply the basic chords completely.

Principle #7: Add variety by displacing a note (or groups of notes) by an octave (moving it up or down).

This note can be moved up one octave for variety.

Exercises for Chord Tone Soloing

Using exercises #1 through #3 in the Appendix, practice each of these "generic" chord shapes over all the basic 13th chord forms: major, dominant, and minor (Cmaj13, C13, and Cm13).

Group 1: Triads on the Root, 3rd, 5th, and 7th

Group 2: 7th Chords on the Root, 3rd, and 5th

Group 3: Descending 7th Chords from the 7th and 9th

Group 4: Ascending/Descending 9th Chords

Group 5: 5-3-1-7 Shapes

Group 6: 7th Chords Starting on Upbeat and Using Triplets (Very Characteristic)

Group 7: 9th Chords Starting on Upbeat and Using Triplets (Very Characteristic)

Group 8: 7th Chords with Chromatic Approach Tones and Triplets

Group 9: 5-3-1-7 Shapes and 9th Chords with Chromatic Approach Tones

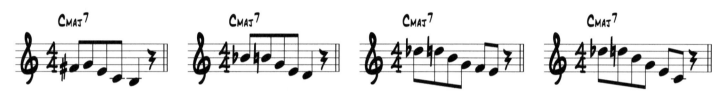

Group 10: 7th and 9th Chords with Double Chromatic Approach Tones

Group 11: 9th Chords with Added Diatonic Passing Chords

The exercises on the previous two pages are an excellent workout, but you probably want to apply them on a song or a progression. Follow the guidelines on the next page once you have a fairly good command of the basic exercises on major 7ths, dominant 7ths, and minor 7ths.

Applying Chord Tone Shapes to a Song or a Progression

1. Prepare a worksheet of the chord tones for each chord. (Make sure you have the correct changes for the tune; don't trust the Internet—it is full of poor and inaccurate versions.) Include altered tones such as ♭9ths, ♯9ths, ♭13ths, ♭5ths, ♯5ths, and ♯11ths.

2. Play the first chord shape in Groups #1 through #5 over each chord in your song (in tempo, with a metronome) until you have them memorized. Avoid writing them out.

3. Play the first chord shape in Groups #6 through #11 over each chord in your song (in tempo, with a metronome) until you have them memorized. Avoid writing them out. These are just ornamented versions of the ones in Groups #1 through #5.

4. Once you can play the first shape in each group from memory and without error, go on to the second shape in each group.

5. Repeat the process for each shape on the list.

6. Pick two shapes that have some contrast and that you like and play them alternately over the progression. Change shapes every other bar.

7. Repeat with two other shapes.

8. Pick shapes at random using your best intuitive judgement. You may find that some lead smoothly into others. Add connecting melodies, using scales or arpeggios as your intuition leads you.

9. Put on a play-along track and improvise. Use the chord shapes as they appear in your mind's ear as something appropriate to play or sing. Incorporate material from Chapters One through Three as your intuition may lead you. Have fun. Don't try to consciously play chord shapes—let them come through organically.

Note: This process may seem laborious, but if you do the preliminary work, you should see results quickly.

Total Package

Using Chord Tone Soloing with Chromatic Approach Tones (CAT) and Diatonic Passing Tones (DPT)

 Demonstration Tracks

Track 22 (Trumpet)

Track 23 (Alto Saxophone)

Track 24 (Vocal)

Track 25 (Rhythm Track)

TOTAL PACKAGE
Using Chord Tone Soloing with Chromatic Approach Tones (CAT)
and Diatonic Passing Tones (DPT)

C Treble Clef Instruments

Mike Steinel

TOTAL PACKAGE

Using Chord Tone Soloing with Chromatic Approach Tones (CAT)
and Diatonic Passing Tones (DPT)

Bb Instruments

Mike Steinel

Total Package

Using Chord Tone Soloing with Chromatic Approach Tones (CAT)
and Diatonic Passing Tones (DPT)

Eb Instruments

Mike Steinel

TOTAL PACKAGE

Using Chord Tone Soloing with Chromatic Approach Tones (CAT)
and Diatonic Passing Tones (DPT)

C Bass Clef Instruments

Mike Steinel

Chapter 7: Ornamenting the Melody of the 3rd

Listen First

- **Dexter Gordon:** "Satin Doll" (*King Neptune*, SteepleChase 1964)

- **Jimmy Heath:** "All the Things You Are" (*On the Trail*, Riverside 1966)

- **Charlie Parker:** "Ornithology" (Savoy 1946)

- **Clifford Brown:** "Donna Lee" (Columbia 1956)

Each Chord Tone Has a Unique Role in the Harmony

Even though jazz musicians may at times emphasize the upper parts of chords (9ths, 11ths, 13ths, and altered tones), the basic structure of harmony lies in the lower chord tones: the root, 3rd, 5th, and 7th. Of these, the 3rd and 7th define the quality (major, minor, dominant) of the chord while the roots provide a foundation and indicate the chord's location. The 5th plays a minor role and is often omitted with little harm to the basic sound of the chord. Only in chords such as the half-diminished 7th (m7b5) does the 5th assume more importance since it is altered.

Color Tones (3rds and 7ths) Define the Quality of the Harmony

Of the two main color tones (the 3rd and 7th), the 3rd is far and away the more powerful, harmonically. Any note can be targeted by ornamentation, but lines that target 3rds produce sounds that imply the harmony most completely.

Two Kinds of 3rds: Major and Minor

There are only two kinds of 3rds: major and minor. In a way, the 3rd represents a "fork in the road." One road points to the major/dominant families, and the other points to the minor family. A melody which uses 3rds clarifies the harmonic path and provides a pleasing and accurate aural image of the song.

The Melody of the 3rd

In a way, the 3rds of the chords, of a progression, make a slow moving melody. We call it the **melody of the 3rd**. Some tunes rely heavily on this melody. "All the Things You Are" by Jerome Kern is almost entirely composed of the 3rds of each chord. "How High the Moon" and "Autumn Leaves" both exploit the 3rds to a large degree.

Good News for Change Runners

The melody of the 3rd is easily remembered and ornamented. Even a beginner, once they have memorized the melody and a few ornaments, can negotiate fairly complex chord progressions with ease. With practice, connecting the 3rd targets will generate authentic jazz melodies that imply the changes.

Downbeats Are Important

The strongest musical forces in melody and rhythm are tension and release. Those forces are at work in every jazz solo. Harmony and meter are bound together and notes on strong beats (such as beat 1 and beat 3 in 4/4 time) have greater harmonic weight that those on weak beats (2 and 4). Ornaments that resolve to strong color tones, like the 3rd on downbeats, can be extremely effective.

How To Practice Color Tone Ornamentation

The charts on the next few pages list the most common ornaments used in jazz solos to target 3rds. (Note: They can be used to target other tones as well). As we outlined in Chapter 5, ornaments can precede targets (approach tones) or follow targets (departure tones). For our purposes, we will start with approach tones since they are the more powerful and a bit tricky at first. Music is like a story and a target tone is like the conclusion of the story (the release of tension). Like a good story that pulls the reader ahead, approach tones introduce tensions which maintain the listener's interest. However, immature improvisers tend to react to chords after they happen, so anticipating, and "thinking ahead" toward a musical goal (like a target note) may seem unnatural at first. Follow the guidelines listed below, and you should feel some improvement in a few sessions.

Practice Guidelines for Approach Tone Ornamentation

1. Pick a progression and memorize the 3rds. Make sure you can play them and sing them. If you need to, write them down on music paper. Start with tunes with one chord per bar or leave out any chord that isn't on beat 1.

2. Pick one simple approach ornament and play it into each 3rd, resolving on beat 1 of the measure, where the chord first appears. Use a metronome or a play-along track.

3. Repeat the same process adding more complicated ornaments as you are able.

4. Pick two and alternate between them.

5. Repeat with various pairs of ornaments.

6. Experiment with adding notes after the target. Use quarter notes at first. Don't worry about the harmonic accuracy of the added notes, but instead, try to connect them to the next approach tone ornament smoothly (avoid awkward leaps).

7. Repeat the same process as #6 but using eighth notes, or eighth-note triplets.

8. Put on a play-along recording and improvise. Play the ornaments and targets as they appear in your mind's ear as being appropriate to the solo. Trust your ears and your intuition.

Diatonic Approach Tones Targeting Major 3rd

Diatonic Approach Tones — Target = Major 3rd

Diatonic Approach Tones Targeting Minor 3rd

Diatonic Approach Tones — Target = Minor 3rd

Chromatic Approach Tones Targeting Major 3rd   **Chromatic Approach Tones Targeting Minor 3rd**

Once you can play a good variety of approach tone ornaments into the 3rds of a progression, the next step is to work on departure tones (tones played "from" or "after" the 3rds). Use the same basic guidelines you did with the approach tones. Some may find this step fairly easy since it overlaps to some degree what you did in Chapter 6.

Practice Guidelines for Departure Tone Ornamentation

1. Pick a progression and memorize the 3rds. Make sure you can play and sing them. If you need to, write them down on music paper. Start with tunes with one chord per bar or leave out any chord that isn't on beat 1.

2. Pick one simple departure ornament and play it from each 3rd, starting on beat 1 of the measure where the chord first appears. Use a metronome or a play-along track.

3. Repeat the same process adding more complicated ornaments as you are able.

4. Pick two and alternate between them.

5. Repeat with various pairs of ornaments.

6. Experiment with the rhythms.

7. Experiment using the reinvention devices discussed in Chapter 1.

8. Put on a play-along recording and improvise. Play the ornaments and targets as they appear in your mind's ear as being appropriate to the solo. Trust your ears and your intuition.

Diatonic Departure Tones from Major 3rd

Diatonic Departure Tones
from Major 3rds

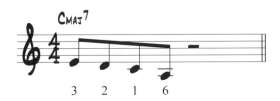

Diatonic Departure Tones from Minor 3rd

Diatonic Departure Tones
from Minor 3rds

Chromatic Departure Tones from Major 3rd

Chromatic Departure Tones
from Major 3rds

Chromatic Departure Tones from Minor 3rd

Chromatic Departure Tones
from Minor 3rds

Connecting Between Ornaments (Putting It All Together)

If you have put in the time reinforcing the approach tones and departure tones on a particular progression, the next step should be relatively easy. If you have gotten to the last step on each list, you probably are already experiencing an improved command of the harmony in your solos. You may find that you can easily connect between the targets.

1. Use the same progression and the worksheet you prepared earlier.

2. Pick one simple approach-tone ornament and combine it with one departure ornament and play them "into" and "out of" each 3rd, keeping the target on beat 1 of the measure where the chord first appears. Use a metronome or a play-along track.

3. Keep the departure tones the same and alternate between different approach tone ornaments.

4. Keep the approach tones the same and alternate between different departure tone ornaments.

5. Pick two or three combinations and alternate between them.

6. Experiment with the rhythms unless the ornaments are four notes long. (When both ornaments are four notes long, they will produce a steady stream of eighth notes.)

7. Experiment delaying the targets so that they land on beats 2 or 3. Avoid putting them on upbeats like the "and" of beat 1 or 2.

8. Put on a play-along recording and improvise. Play the ornaments and targets as they appear in your mind's ear as being appropriate to the solo. Trust your ears and your intuition.

This Is Hard but Important Work

Caution: In the beginning, this can be very taxing, intellectually. If you are having to think through everything, limit your practice sessions on a paticular tune to ten or 15 minute segments. After your intuition takes over and you can "feel" your way through the 3rds, you can increase the time of your practice segments and work more on style, tone, time accuracy, time feel, articulations, and other expressive elements.

Studying Transcriptions Will Help

Listen to recordings and study transcriptions. Try to find the target notes and notice how the great players get into and out of them. You will see many of the ornaments we have talked about in this chapter and many new ones. Keep a notebook of favorites. As you get more confident with each, let your ear take over and work to weave your way into and out of the target notes as smoothly as possible. With diligent daily work you should experience a new freedom in creating melodies. Enjoy!

Jerry's Song

Targeting the Melody of the 3rd

 Demonstration Tracks

Track 26 (Trumpet)

Track 27 (Alto Saxophone)

Track 28 (Trombone)

Track 29 (Guitar)

Track 30 (Vocal)

Track 31 (Rhythm Track)

Jerry's Song
Targeting the Melody of the 3rd

C Treble Clef Instruments

Mike Steinel

JERRY'S SONG

Targeting the Melody of the 3rd

Bb Instruments

Mike Steinel

Jerry's Song
Targeting the Melody of the 3rd

Mike Steinel

Eb Instruments

JERRY'S SONG
Targeting the Melody of the 3rd

C Bass Clef Instruments

Mike Steinel

Chapter 8: Scale/Mode Theory

The term "mode" is just another name for "scale." A scale is a group of notes (usually between five and eight notes) arranged in combinations of half steps, whole steps, and sometimes augmented steps. Each scale or mode has a unique flavor that will sound "in unity" (sound "good with" or "like") a chord type.

The Six Basic Scale/Mode Families

There are six basic scale environments (or families) that most are most commonly used in jazz: the major scale, the harmonic minor scale, the ascending melodic minor scale, the whole tone scale, the diminished scale, and the harmonic major scale. We have discussed the blues scales in Level One and will discuss pentatonic scales in Level Three. Here are the six basic scale/mode environments:

C Major Scale

C Harmonic Minor Scale

C Melodic Minor Scale (Ascending)

C Whole Tone Scale

C Diminished Scale

C Harmonic Major Scale

Each of these scale/mode families can generate different (but closely related) modes by starting on and emphasizing different notes. The most common of the scales, the major scale generates seven modes.

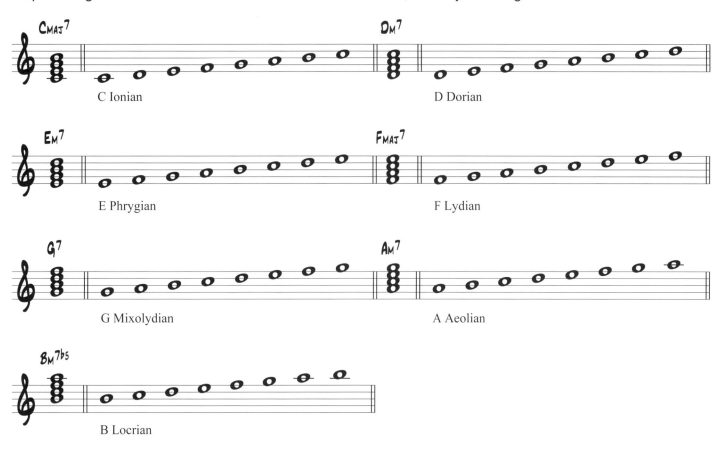

Music theorists have assigned names to each of the modes of the major scale. For most of the other exotic scales, the modes are simply labeled with a number. (The one exception is melodic minor.) When a note name precedes the number of a mode, it indicates the starting note of the mode. If it follows the number, it indicates the first note of the parent mode. For example: "D 2nd Mode, Harmonic Minor" and "2nd Mode of C Harmonic Minor" are two names for the same mode.

The harmonic minor scale generates seven modes.

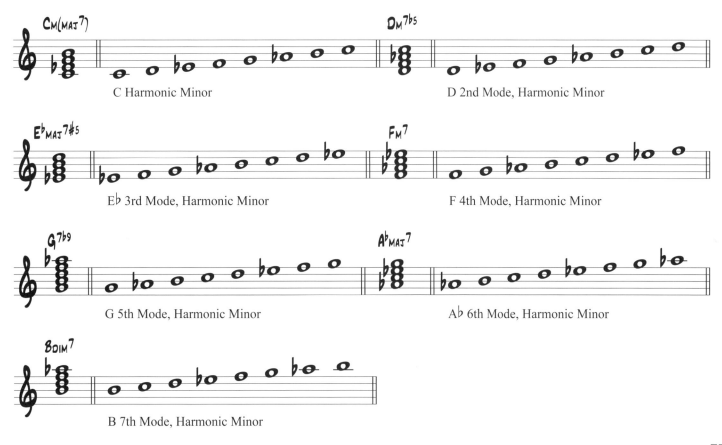

The ascending melodic minor scale (usually referred to as melodic minor) has seven modes.

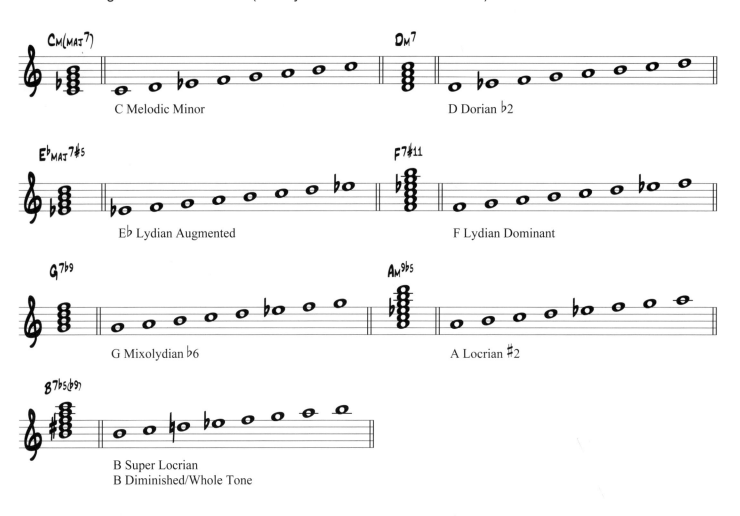

C Melodic Minor

D Dorian ♭2

E♭ Lydian Augmented

F Lydian Dominant

G Mixolydian ♭6

A Locrian ♯2

B Super Locrian
B Diminished/Whole Tone

The harmonic major scale has seven modes.

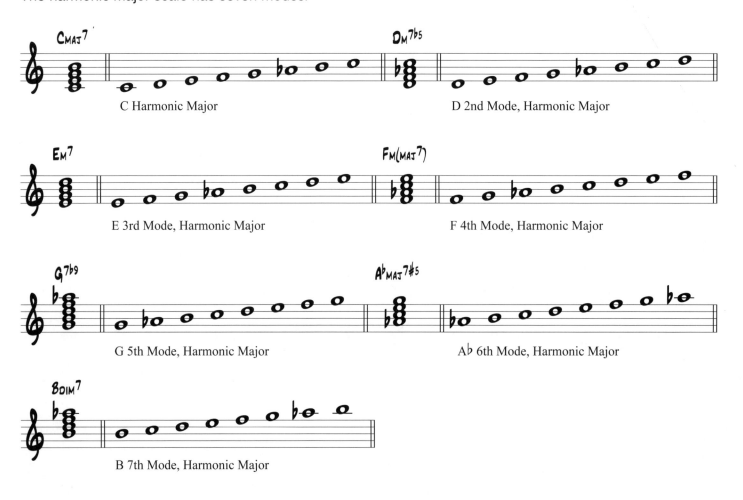

C Harmonic Major

D 2nd Mode, Harmonic Major

E 3rd Mode, Harmonic Major

F 4th Mode, Harmonic Major

G 5th Mode, Harmonic Major

A♭ 6th Mode, Harmonic Major

B 7th Mode, Harmonic Major

The whole tone scale has one unique mode. The diminished scale has two unique modes.

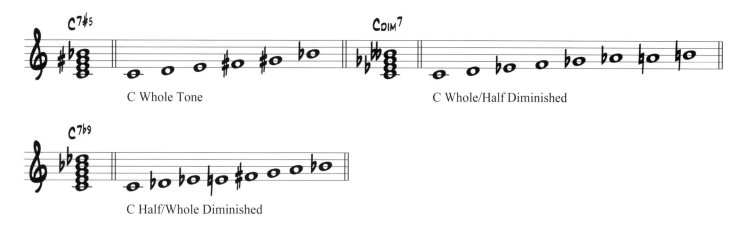

C Whole Tone   C Whole/Half Diminished

C Half/Whole Diminished

Although the number and variety of modes on the preceding page may seem overwhelming, students will be pleased to know that most jazz improvisers use only a handful of the most effective scales and modes. The first list below includes the six most commonly used scales/modes and the chords they imply or "sound in unity with." They are arranged in an order determined by their frequency of occurrence. Most jazz songs can be negotiated artistically with these sounds.

The Six Most Common Modes/Scales in Jazz

C Mixolydian (Fifth Mode of Major Scale)

C Dorian (Second Mode of Major Scale)

C Ionian (First Mode of Major Scale)

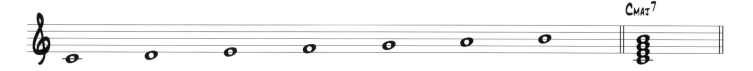

C Fifth Mode, Harmonic Minor (from F Harmonic Minor)

C Fifth Mode, Harmonic Major (from F Harmonic Major)

C Locrian (Seventh Mode of Major Scale)

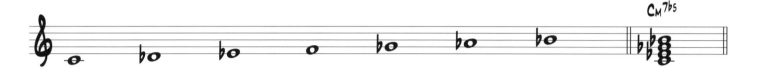

Here are three more exotic scales/modes which can be used to improvise for more advanced material.

C Whole Tone Scale

C Locrian #2 (Sixth Mode of Melodic Minor)

C Half/Whole Diminished

Basic Exercises for Mixolydian, Dorian, and Ionian Modes

These three modes are derived from the major scale and are the most common modes needed to apply to the ii–V–I progression in major keys. Practice each mode from all 12 chromatic notes.

Mixolydian (Fifth Mode of the Major Scale) w/ Arpeggio

Continue practicing this exercise, moving from all 12 starting notes.

Dorian (Second Mode of the Major Scale) w/ Arpeggio

Continue practicing this exercise, moving from all 12 starting notes.

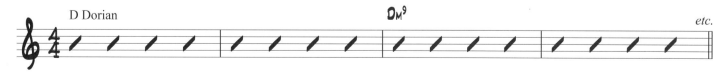

Ionian (Fifth Mode of the Major Scale) w/ Arpeggio

Continue practicing this exercise, moving from all 12 starting notes.

Basic Exercises for Fifth Mode of Harmonic Minor, Fifth Mode of Harmonic Major, and Locrian (Seventh Mode of Major)

These three modes are derived from the harmonic minor scale, the harmonic major scale, and the major scale. They are the most commonly used modes applied to ii–V–I progressions in minor keys.

Harmonic Minor, Fifth Mode w/ Arpeggio

Continue practicing this exercise, moving from all 12 starting notes.

Harmonic Major, Fifth Mode w/ Arpeggio

Continue practicing this exercise, moving from all 12 starting notes.

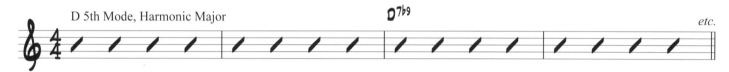

Locrian (Seventh Mode of Major) w/ Arpeggio

Continue practicing this exercise, moving from all 12 starting notes.

Chapter 9: Scale/Mode Soloing

Listen First

- Miles Davis (w/ John Coltrane): "So What" (*Kind of Blue*, Columbia 1959)

- Miles Davis (w/ John Coltrane): "All Blues" (*Kind of Blue*, Columbia 1959)

- John Coltrane: "Pursuance" (*A Love Supreme*, Impulse 1965)

- Horace Silver: "Sister Sadie" (*Blowin' the Blues Away*, Blue Note 1959)

- Lee Morgan: "The Sidewinder" (*The Sidewinder*, Blue Note 1963)

Definitions

- **Modal Approach**: Soloing that emphasizes scale tones more than chord tones.

- **Vamps**: Extended sections of repeated chords.

- **Scale Bracketing**: Using one scale over multiple chords.

Using scales in jazz soloing is particularly useful in the following situations:

1. When a chord progression has long sections of one or two chords.

D Dorian Melody

2. When a progression has groups of chords that are closely related in one key and are in such quick succession that applying a unique mode or arpeggio for each chord is impractical. This is often a successful approach when soloing over vamps (intro or ending vamps).

C Major Melody

3. When a performer intends to construct a melody that purposely avoids implying each individual change.

B♭ Major Melody

It is possible, but perhaps not advisable, to approach every chord with a different scale or mode. The example below illustrates how cumbersome this approach could be on a chord progression that moves quickly and shifts between keys.

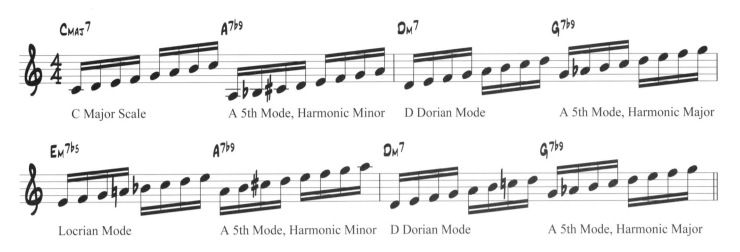

There are some chords that have slower moving (and more repetitive) chord progressions that lend themselves well to using one scale for each chord.

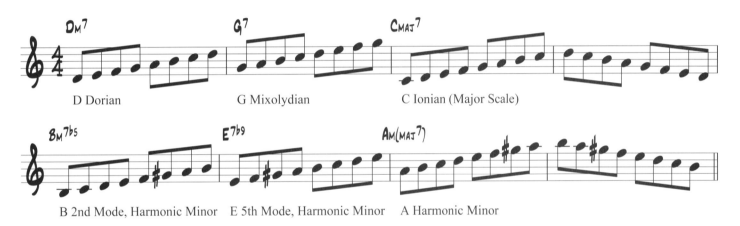

At times, players may choose to use one scale over many chords that are in the same key. This technique is called scale bracketing and can be useful; however, there is a risk that the generalized scale may inadvertently inject dissonant notes over some chords. In the example below, the C major scale in the first bar fails to suggest the first chord but works well over the 2nd and 3rd. The key to achieving harmonic clarity with scale bracketing is to adjust the scale to maintain chord tones on downbeats.

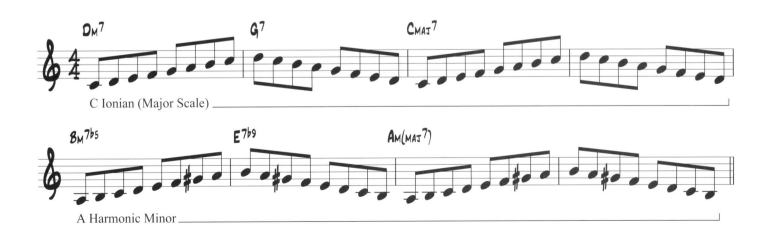

This example of scale bracketing uses two scales and does a better job of implying the harmony of the first and third chord. However, since it has chord tones of the second chord landing on upbeats, it doesn't imply the correct sound. In a fast tempo, this may not be an issue, but at a slow or medium tempo, the listener may feel a sense that the melody doesn't really fit or "sound in unity" with the chord.

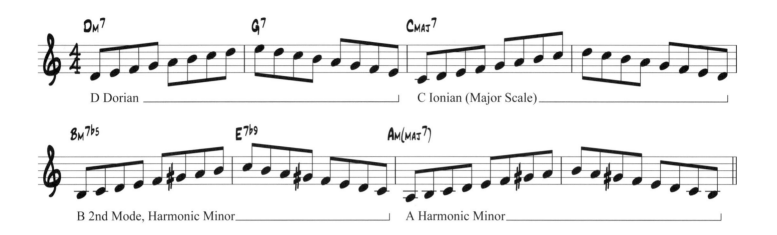

Making Scales Interesting

Although running scales can produce an accurate implication of the harmony, just running up and down a scale will not produce interesting melodies. A scale is just an "alphabet" in a way, and an alphabet needs words to become a vocabulary. Jazz musicians break scales up into small units of melodies which can be thought of as words or cells. Just as cells in a body work together to make bigger organisms, scale cells can be combined in interesting ways to build strong melodies.

The chart below contains 12 very common cells constructed with scale tones. They make a large part of the vocabulary found in jazz improvisations. The exercises on the next page apply each of these 12 cells to all the notes of the C major scale. Practice them in all 12 major scales first, then apply them to the six most common modes/scales listed in Chapter 8: the Mixolydian mode, the Dorian mode, the major scale (Ionian mode), the fifth mode of harmonic minor, the fifth mode of harmonic minor, and the Locrian mode.

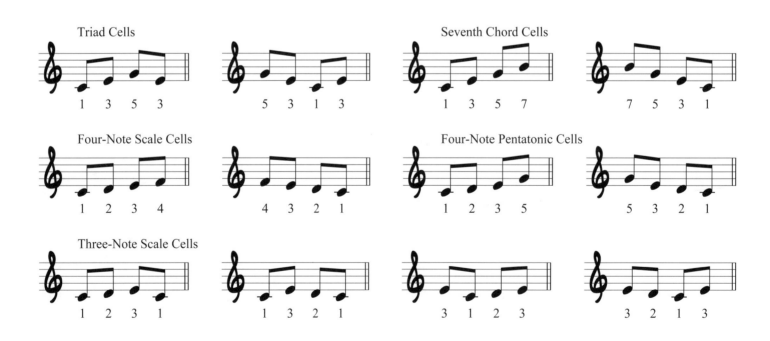

Basic Scale Cells Applied to the C Major Scale

Daylight Savings

Using Modes

Demonstration Tracks

Track 32 (Trumpet)

Track 33 (Tenor Saxophone)

Track 34 (Vocal)

Track 35 (Rhythm Track)

Daylight Savings
Using Modes

C Treble Clef Instruments

Mike Steinel

Daylight Savings
Using Modes

B♭ Instruments

Mike Steinel

Daylight Savings
Using Modes

Eb Instruments

Mike Steinel

91

Daylight Savings
Using Modes

C Bass Clef Instruments

Mike Steinel

Level Three

Level Two of *Running the Changes* introduced students to three improvisation skills: chord tone soloing, ornamenting the melody of the 3rd, and scale mode soloing. It also provided the basic theoretical information needed to apply those techniques effectively. Once again, these appear in most jazz solos by mature improvisers. Armed with the information in Level Two, you should be able to improvise or compose solos that imply the changes (or progression) of most songs. Your results should be accurate harmonically, but you might feel they lack the harmonic nuances you hear in the solos you admire.

Level Two dealt with the sound of each chord in a progression as an isolated event. Level Three delves into a deeper discussion of how chords relate to one another. Each chord has a relationship with the other chords around it and the general key of a song. The term we use for that relationship is **function**. The relationship between chords is closely related to how the individual tones of each chord move as a new chord is introduced. This is often referred to as **voice leading**. In order for a progression to sound logical, some chord tones must move smoothly into the next chord. That motion is called **resolution**. Chapter 11, in particular, is about the strongest resolution in jazz music: the **7-to-3 resolution**. The 7-to-3 resolution is the skeletal framework that connects chord tones as the roots of those chords move up in 4ths or down 5ths. That root motion is the most common in jazz from the Bebop era to the present day and is the basic structure of the **ii–V–I progression**. Chapter 12 presents the **bebop scale** and its variations that make the execution of eighth notes over the ii–V–I progression profoundly easier. Chapter 13 focuses on **advanced color tone ornamentation** and provides the theoretical information necessary to understand the final three topics of Level Three: advanced color tone ornamentation, **altered dominant scales**, and **pentatonic and hexatonic scales**.

As you explore these chapters, practice the exercises and play through the etudes, you may begin to feel that your solos sound a bit more modern or sophisticated. That's the intent. Please remember to review and work to ingrain the material in Levels One and Two. In particular, keep training your ear and your intuition: *Play with recordings—play with recordings a lot!* One of the dangers we face is that as we begin to rely more on our intellect, we may in effect "turn off our ears."

Level Three Outline

Chapter 10: Chord Function and Basic Progressions

Chapter 11: Ornamenting the 7-to-3 Resolution

Chapter 12: Using Bebop Scales

Chapter 13: Advanced Color Tone Ornamentation

Chapter 14: Using Altered Dominant Scales

Chapter 15: Pentatonics and Hexatonics

Chapter 10: Chord Function and Basic Progressions

Playing improvised melodies that successfully "run" the changes requires an understanding of how chords function in a progression. Here are the basic principles of chord function:

1. Most jazz progressions are organized in keys. Most start in a "main" key and modulate (or shift) to other keys for harmonic variety.

2. Chords can be constructed on each note of the key (or scale).

3. Chords within a key will have different qualities (major, minor, dominant, half-diminished, or diminished).

4. Chord quality is consistent between keys. For example, all chords built on the first note of major keys are major seventh in quality.

5. Chords in a key are labeled (generically) using Roman numerals.

Summary: Chords function in a key and are labeled by the location of the root of each chord. For example, the I chord is built on the first note of the parent scale (key note), the ii chord is built on the second note of the scale, and so on.

Chords in the Key of C Major

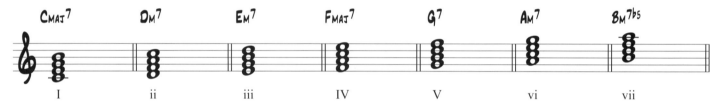

The term "function" is another way to explain a chord's basic job. There are two general jobs for chords: "moving or resting," or in musical terms, "tension or release." Here is a summary of how chords work (or function) in major keys:

Chord Label	Quality	Function	Possible Motion
I	Major 7th	Establishes Key	Doesn't need to move but may go anywhere
ii	Minor 7th	Tension	Resolves up a 4th to V
ii	Minor 7th	Substitutes for I	Resolves up to vi
IV	Major 7th	Substitutes for ii	Resolves up to V
V	Dominant 7th	Tension	Resolves down to I
vi	Minor 7th	Substitutes for I	Resolves up to ii
vii	m7♭5	Substitutes for V	Resolves up to I

94

You will notice that four of the seven basic chords act mainly as substitutes for one of the more important chords: I, ii, and V. Most jazz progressions can be reduced to some combination of I, ii, or V chords.

Chords in minor keys have similar functions. Generally, the Roman numeral labeling is adjusted to show how it relates to the parallel major key.

Chords in the Key of C Harmonic Minor

Chord Label	Quality	Function	Possible Motion
i	Minor 7th	Establishes Key	Doesn't need to move but can
ii	Minor 7♭5	Tension	Resolves up a 4th to V
♭III	Major 7th	Substitutes for i	Resolves up to VI
iv	Minor 7th	Substitutes for ii	Resolves up to V
V	Dominant 7♭9	Tension	Resolves down to i
♭VI	Major 7th	Substitutes for I	Resolves up to ii
VII	°7	Substitutes for V	Resolves up to i

Common Jazz Progressions

Although the possible combinations of chords in jazz tunes might seem to be infinite, most mainstream jazz tunes use just a few very common combinations. The most common is the ii–V–I progression. The second most common is the I–vi–ii–V.

Chords in the Key of C Major

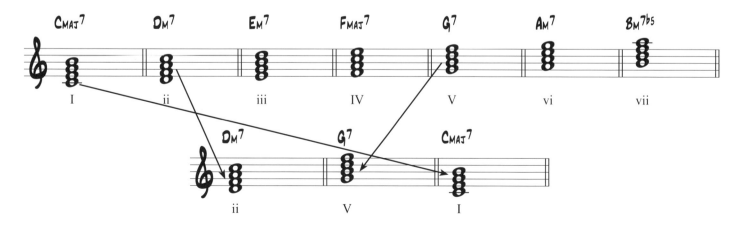

It is important that jazz improvisers learn to recognize the ii–V–I progression when learning tunes. There are 12 major keys and 12 chord combinations for the ii–V–I in major.

- Key of C Major (Dm7–G7–Cmaj7)
- Key of D♭ Major (E♭m7–A♭7–D♭maj7)
- Key of D Major (Em7–A7–Dmaj7)
- Key of E♭ Major (Fm7–B♭7–E♭maj7)
- Key of E Major (F#m7–B7–Emaj7)
- Key of F Major (Gm7–C7–Fmaj7)
- Key of G♭ Major (A♭m7–D♭7–G♭maj7)
- Key of G Major (Am7–D7–Gmaj7)
- Key of A♭ Major (B♭m7–E♭7–A♭maj7)
- Key of A Major (Bm7–E7–Amaj7)
- Key of B♭ Major (Cm7–F7–B♭maj7)
- Key of B Major (C#m7–F#7–Bmaj7)

The ii–V–I in a minor key has the same root motion as the ii–V–I in a major key, but the qualities of the individual chords are different. The ii chord is half-diminished, the V chord has an altered (usually lowered) 9th, and the i chord has a lowered 3rd and a natural 7th.

Chords in the Key of C Harmonic Minor

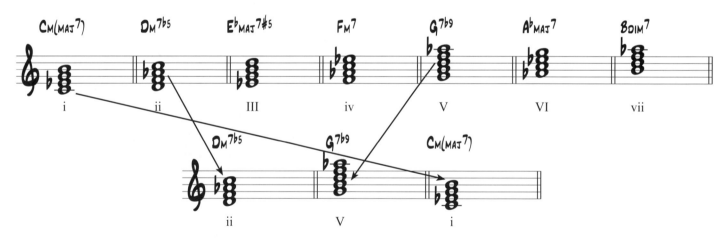

Most jazz progressions will modulate at least once. The progression below modulates to the relative minor key.

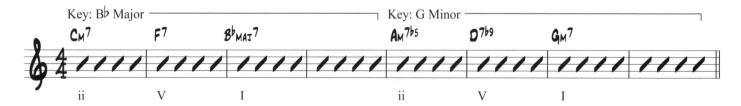

Often, progressions will use only the ii and V of the ii–V–I. A major 7th by itself usually will establish the feeling of a key center.

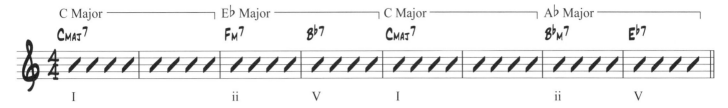

The ii–V progression is commonly one or two bars long.

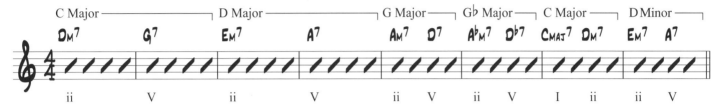

Improving Basic Progressions

To generate more harmonic interest and motion, jazz improvisers will often insert ii–V–Is or ii–Vs into simple progressions.

Typical Basic Progression

Same Progression with Added ii–Vs

Jazz composers and improvisers typically mix the major and minor versions of basic progressions to achieve variety. Typically, the V7b9 chord from the minor key is often substituted for the blander V7 from the parallel major.

ii–V–I in C Major

ii–V–I in C Minor

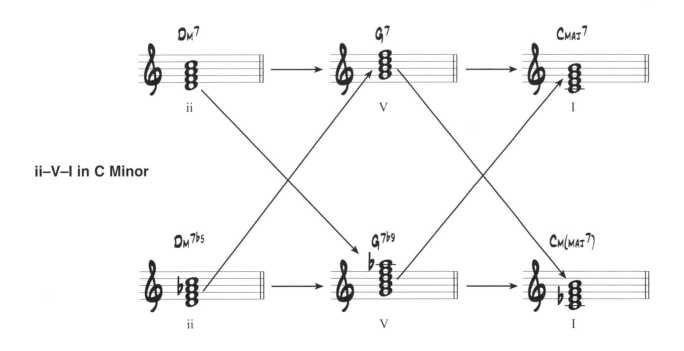

Chapter 11: Ornamenting the 7-to-3 Resolution

Listen First

- Clifford Brown: "Pent Up House" (*Sonny Rollins Plus Four*, Prestige 1956)

- Blue Mitchell: "Stablemates" (*Stablemates*, Candid 1977)

- Sonny Stitt: "Scrapple from the Apple" (*Stitt Plays Bird*, Atlantic 1963)

Definitions

- **Resolution**: The melodic motion connecting chords from tension to relaxation.

- **Guide Tone Melody**: A melody generated by resolving tones.

The most common root motion in jazz progressions is up a 4th (same as down a 5th). For example: The ii chord usually moves to V, the V chord usually moves to I, and the vi chord often moves to ii. The strongest resolving motion when chords move up a 4th is the 7th of the first chord moves down by step to the 3rd of the second chord. In a typical piano voicing of a ii–V–I (see below), the roots move up in 4ths move (or down in 5ths) and the 7ths will resolve (by step) to 3rds. No other motion will happen.

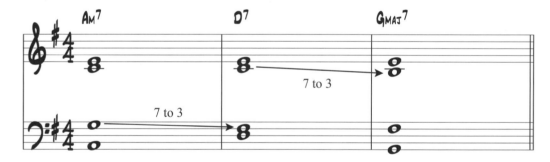

Using the 7-to-3 Without Ornamentation

Even without ornamentation, the 7-to-3 resolution sounds complete and melodically satisfying. The song "Tea for Two" uses 7-to-3 as its basic melodic motif. Often, when the changes are very quick, a simple rhythmic statement of the 7-to-3 can be effective.

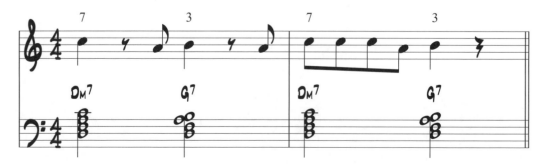

Ornamenting the 7-to-3—"Three In/Two Out"

Using the 7-to-3 as a basic melody to which ornamentation can be added has been a very common in jazz "change running" since the 1940s. I suggest a simple of method of ornamentation, which I call "Three In/Two Out."

Three In/Two Out Explained

1. Think of the 7-to-3 as a "doorway" through which our melodies must pass if we want the listener to hear that a ii–V has happened.

2. There are three melodies over the ii chord that all take us to the doorway (to the 7th).

   A. 1-3-5-7, (Root, 3rd, 5th, and 7th of the ii chord)

   B. 3-2-1-7 (3rd, 2nd, Root, and 7th of the ii chord)

   C. 5-3-1-7 (5th, 3rd, Root, and 7th of the ii chord)

3. There are two melodies over the V chord that each take us out of the doorway (from the 3rd).

   A. 3-5-7-9 (3rd, 5th, 7th, and 9th of the V Chord)

   B. 3-2-1-7 (3rd, 2nd, Root, and 7th of the V Chord)

4. These melodies can be applied to ii–Vs in major and minor keys (with some accidentals).

5. The three "ins" can be combined with any of the two "outs" to make six "raw" patterns.

6. The raw patterns can be ornamented and reinvented in a number of ways.

   A. Notes can be added in front, in back, or in the middle of the raw patterns.

   B. Octave displacement of parts of any pattern can be used to disguise the melody.

   C. They can be played in any rhythmic sub-division that is appropriate to the music.

   D. They may be truncated, with many notes left out.

E. Octave displacement is common to avoid extreme registers. The two most common octave displacements are in the ways out. The last three notes of the first way out are often dropped down an octave, and the last three notes of the second way out are often played an octave higher.

Here are the six raw patterns in eighth notes for major and minor keys. They are written in the key of C. Practice them each over practice progressions #4 and #5 in the Appendix.

Raw Patterns in Major   **Raw Patterns in Minor**

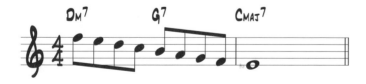 

The 7-to-3 Melody Over the ii and V Chords

This is a very important thing to remember: The 7-to-3 melody sounds well over the ii and V chords. Each of the patterns works equally well over an isolated ii7 or V7. Therefore, they can be played anywhere during the duration of the ii–V7 progression.

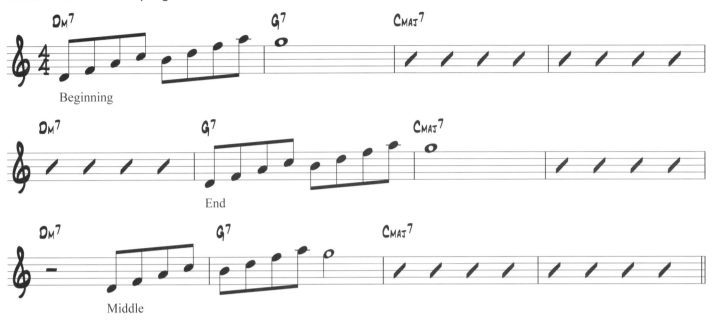

The basic patterns may be disguised by adding ornamentations. Here are some common ornamentations of Three-In/Two-Out patterns.

Notes can be added to the front and back of basic patterns.

Passing tones can be added between the notes of the basic patterns.

Notes can be inserted between the 7th and 3rd.

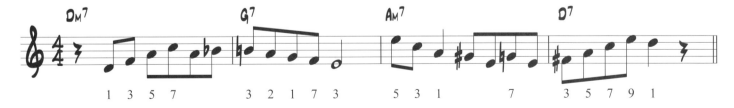

Patterns can be truncated by leaving notes off from the beginning or the end of the phrase.

Often, two or more patterns are combined.

Be careful with the second way out; it can sound awkward if it resolves to the 3rd of the tonic chord too soon.

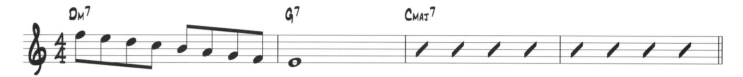

A common solution is to add a passing tone so that the pattern lands on the 7th of the V chord.

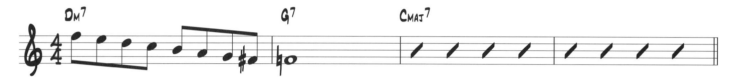

Practice Guidelines for Ornamenting the 7-to-3 Resolution

Practice the raw patterns in all 12 keys before trying to "plug" them in on a tune. Try to master them in eighth notes at a fairly fast tempo so you are forced to think (and hear) them as one small complete sentence, not as separate notes. After some diligent practice, you should begin to incorporate them into your lines without being too obvious. Study transcriptions for ideas on how to add ornamentation, displace them rhythmically, and truncate them. In songs with extended ii–V7s or extended vamps over Mixolydian and Dorian modes, you may find it easy to fire off two or three 7-to-3 sentences in a row. For more on this topic, consult Bert Ligon's *Connecting Chords with Linear Harmony*.

Some Things to Avoid: (Common Tendencies of New Players)

1. Don't overuse the same raw pattern beginning on beat 1. Instead, use rhythmic displacement to add variety. Use approach tone ornamentation, leading into the first note of the Three-In/Two-Out pattern and try to start on upbeats.

2. Don't play the same pattern over sequential ii–V7s. It is too obvious—mix it up.

Up next is a sample solo that exploits the 7-to-3 resolution over the changes to a very common bebop standard. See if you can recognize ways in and out. The 7ths and 3rds are labeled.

Scufflin' with McGuffin

Using Ornamentation of the 7-to-3

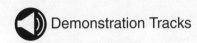 Demonstration Tracks

Track 36 (Trumpet)

Track 37 (Tenor Saxophone)

Track 38 (Vocal)

Track 39 (Rhythm Track)

Scufflin' with McGuffin
Using Ornamentation of the 7-to-3

C Treble Clef Instruments

Mike Steinel

Scufflin' with McGuffin
Using Ornamentation of the 7-to-3

B♭ Instruments

Mike Steinel

SCUFFLIN' WITH MCGUFFIN
Using Ornamentation of the 7-to-3

Eb Instruments

Mike Steinel

SCUFFLIN' WITH MCGUFFIN
Using Ornamentation of the 7-to-3

C Bass Clef Instruments

Mike Steinel

Chapter 12: Bebop Scale Soloing

Listen First

- Charlie Parker; "Ornithology" (Dial 1946)

- Fats Navarro: "Ladybird" (*Prime Source*, Bluenote 1948)

- Clifford Brown: "Cherokee" (*Study in Brown*, Emarcy 1955)

- Freddie Hubbard: "Birdlike" (*Hub-Tones*, Blue Note 1962)

- Blue Mitchell: "Scrapple from the Apple" (*Blue Moods*, Riverside 1960)

- Tom Harrell: "Unit Seven" (w/ John McNeil) (*Look to the Sky*, SteepleChase 1979)

Definitions

- **Bebop**: A style of jazz which originated in the 1940s and highlighted chromaticism.

- **Bebop Scales**: Scales generated by adding extra notes to basic modes and scales.

Extra Notes in Bebop Scales

Eighth-note rhythms are a central feature of jazz soloing in the bebop style, but creating solos in eighth notes is difficult if you are only using seven note scales. Melodies can be awkward and "unbalanced." Early beboppers such as Charlie Parker and Dizzy Gillespie drew heavily from swing players such as Lester Young and Roy Eldridge, both of whom were masters at adding "extra notes." However, Bird and Dizzy Gillespie (among others) took it quite a few steps further. Much later, jazz educators codified these melodic constructions and gave them the label "bebop scales." The work of David Baker and Barry Harris is the most significant in this area.

In his book *How to Play Bebop*, David Baker identifies four bebop scales. They each have a distinct harmonic application and are built by adding one extra note to a basic mode of the major scale.

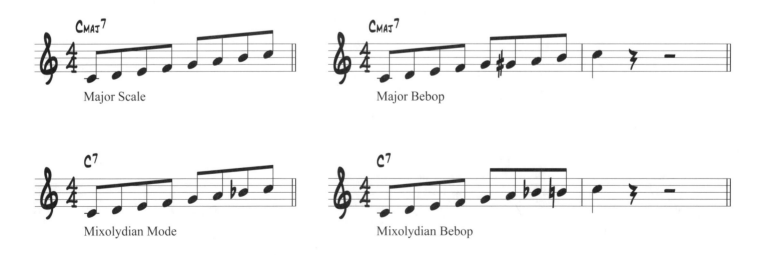

To make our work a bit easier, it is useful to note that three of the above scales are actually modes of each other. The Mixolydian, Dorian, and Locrian bebop scales are built from the same construction. There is a similar connection between their related chords. In the chart below, there are three chords: C7, Gm7, and Em7♭5. If C7 is a V7 chord, then the Gm7 is its related ii7 chord (a very common grouping in bebop jazz). Em7♭5 can be thought of as being the top part of a C9 chord.

Using the Scales in Solos

Like everything in jazz, bebop scales are best learned through modeling (listening and imitation). Practicing the raw scales is helpful, but drawing bebop scale vocabulary from solos will be more effective. Charlie Parker is considered one of the chief inventors of bebop, and his solos are loaded with "bebop scale" melodies. Sonny Stitt, John Coltrane (early career), Miles Davis, Cannonball Adderley, Blue Mitchell, and Freddie Hubbard are also great resources.

Some Helpful Hints about Bebop Scales

Bebop scales make it easier to build jazz lines which have rhythmic and harmonic stability. Remember these simple principles (from David Baker's *How To Play Bebop*): When bebop scale lines are started with a chord tone on a downbeat (remember, the 6th is a chord tone on the major bebop scale) and played in eighth notes, chord tones will be maintained on downbeats and the melodies produced will imply the underlying harmony.

If the line starts on a chord tone, stays within the bebop scale, and remains in eighth notes, chord tones will be maintained on downbeats. Regardless of any change of direction, chord tones will continue to land on strong beats (1, 2, 3, or 4 in 4/4) presenting a clear implication of the harmony.

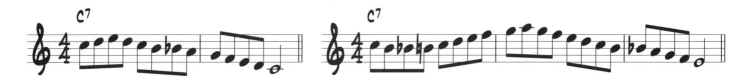

If the line needs to start on a non-chord tone, one of the following must happen to regain harmonic balance:

Starting the Bebop Scale on Non-Chord Tones

Beginning on an Upbeat

Playing a Quarter Note First

Leaving out the First "Extra" Note

Adding a Chromatic Passing Tone

Playing a Syncopated Figure

Getting Started with Bebop Scales

Before attempting to use bebop scales in solos, it is important to gain a certain amount of facility with the raw scales. Practice the scales up and down form each chord tone.

For more bebop scale exercises, check out my book *Building a Jazz Vocabulary*.

Focus on the Bebop Part of Each Scale

When trying to incorporate bebop scales into a song it may be helpful to begin by focusing on the spot in each scale that has the extra notes (8-7-♭7 for Mixolydian and 5-♯5-6 for major). Try running down from the root on the Mixolydian and up from the 5th on majors. Remember: The Dorian and Mixolydian are modes of each other so you can take every ii–V7 and reduce it to a V7 chord. Next up is an example of the work procedure over the changes to "Ornithology" (first eight bars).

Starting Phrases

Continuous Eighth-Note Motion

Once you are comfortable with the basic notes of each scale, work to turn it into music through rhythmic displacement, use of space, and phrasing.

Bebop Scale Variation #1: Adding Notes

It is common that extra notes are added to the basic bebop scales. Barry Harris made a thorough study of these commonly added extra notes, which generally consist of additional chromatic passing notes between the 3rd and root of both the Mixolydian bebop scale and the major bebop scale. Below are just a few of the common combinations. Jerry Bergonzi calls these "ten-note bebop scales."

Adding Chromatic Passing Tones Between the 3rd and Root to Mixolydian Bebop

Adding Chromatic Passing Tones Between the 3rd and Root to Major Bebop

Adding Chromatic Passing Tones Between the 3rd and 2nd to Mixolydian

Bebop Scale Variation #2: Adding Bebop Scales to Harmonic Major and Minor

It is also very common for improvisors to add altered tones to the basic Mixolydian bebop scale. In a way, this will produce hybrids that are bebop but also harmonic minor or harmonic major.

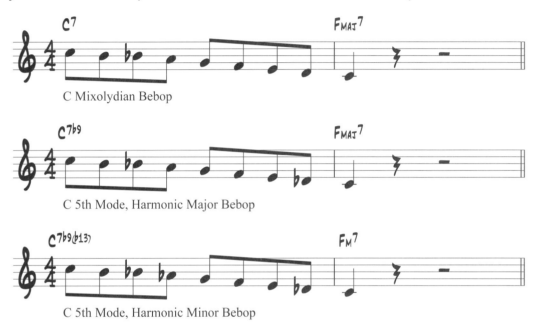

The following patterns use bebop scales to outline the ii–V–I progression. Practice them in all 12 keys over practice progression #4 in the Appendix.

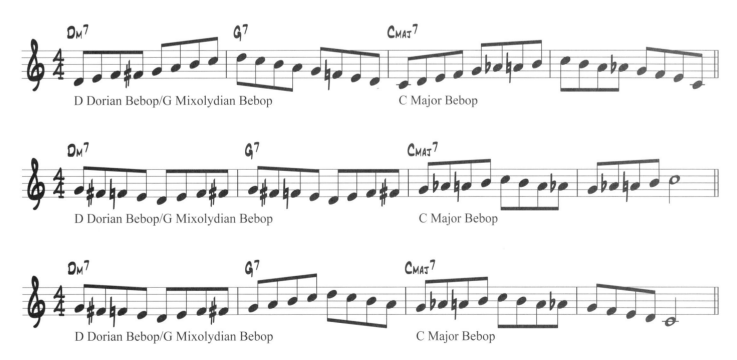

Birdwatching

Using Bebop Scales

Demonstration Tracks

Track 40 (Trumpet)

Track 41 (Tenor Saxophone)

Track 42 (Vocal)

Track 43 (Rhythm Track)

BIRDWATCHING
Using Bebop Scales

C Treble Clef Instruments

Mike Steinel

BIRDWATCHING
Using Bebop Scales

Bb Instruments

Mike Steinel

BIRDWATCHING
Using Bebop Scales

Eb Instruments

Mike Steinel

BIRDWATCHING
Using Bebop Scales

C Bass Clef Instruments

Mike Steinel

Chapter 13: Advanced Color Tone Ornamentation

Listen First

- Charlie Parker: "Yardbird Suite" (Dial, 1946)

- John Coltrane: "'Round Midnight" (*Round About Midnight*, Columbia 1957)

- Sonny Rollins: "Moritat" (*Saxophone Colossus*, Prestige 1956)

- Blue Mitchell: "I'll Close My Eyes" (*Blue Moods*, Riverside 1960)

Definitions

- **Home Key**: The basic key of a song—usually starts and ends in this key.

- **Color Tones**: 3rds, 7ths, and altered tones of chords.

- **Non-Diatonic Color Tones**: Color tones not belonging to the main "home" key of a song.

"It's just music. It's playing clean and looking for the pretty notes."
–Charlie Parker

In previous chapters, we have explored the use of the two basic color tones: the 3rd and the 7th. In particular, we stressed ornamenting the melody of the 3rd. Restricting our ornamentation to the 3rd will present a clear picture of the harmony, but it may result in a melody that is repetitious and boring. In general, if the 3rds and 7ths are in the home key, it may be more interesting to find other notes to ornament.

Other Important Color Tones

- **The flatted 5th** of half diminished chords (m7♭5)

- **Roots or 9ths** of any chord (can provide surprise and variety)

- **Altered (raised or lowered) 9ths and 5ths** (♭9, ♯9, ♭5, ♯5) of dominant 7ths (V7)

The second melody (on the next page) has more potential to be interesting since it doesn't return to the same tones so often and stresses some altered tones. Sometimes, the root is an effective note to ornament.

Targets: 3   3   ♭5   3   ♭5   7   ♭9   Root

Hint: Once you have mastered the melody of the 3rd of a progression, look for the places to add altered notes. Remember: When the 3rd or 7th of a chord doesn't belong to the home key, it should be emphasized or at least included in your line. Studying solos by great change runners will reveal that principle quite clearly.

The Most Important Chords

The most important chords of a tune progression (those that make it unique) are the chords that are non-diatonic to the key. Effective change running will exploit those non-diatonic sounds by emphasizing their basic color tones (3rd or 7th), emphasizing an altered 5th or 9th, or, in some cases, emphasizing the root or 5th. The melody of the song often reveals clues as to the best notes to ornament. Play through the example below and observe how the second melody suggests the harmony more completely than the first.

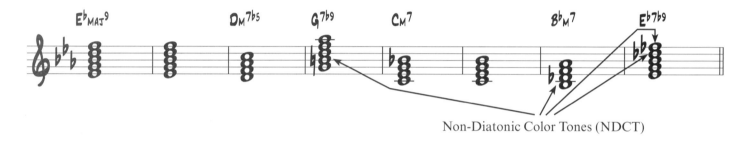

Non-Diatonic Color Tones (NDCT)

These melodies fit the changes, but they are rather bland.

These melodies are harmonically stronger.

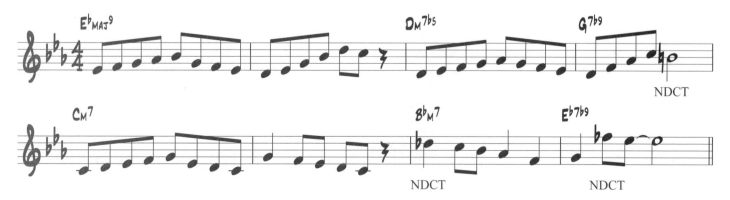

Three Important Advanced Principles in Change Running

Principle #1: Alter the Dominants That Resolve Up a 4th

Since the Bebop era, mature players generally alter dominants that resolve to I, even if the chord progression doesn't indicate an alteration. The most common alteration is the ♭9, but #9, ♭5, and #5 are possible. The melody of 3-to-♭9 on V7 chords is very expressive and resolves convincingly. (Add the ♭9 to V7 chords that resolve up a 4th.)

Using exotic scales with resolving dominants is an effective technique. Diminished (half-whole), diminished whole tone, and the fifth modes of harmonic minor and harmonic major work well.

Principle #2: ii and V Chords Work as a Team

The ii and V chords are unique in that they in do a similar job, which is to add tension before returning or resolving to I (up a 4th/down a 5th). In a way, they are slightly different colorations of the same sort of tension. This is good news for the improviser since it means that progressions can be simplified (by removing the ii or the V) or made more complicated (by adding a ii or a V).

Basic Progression with Various ii–Vs

Basic Progression with ii–Vs Simplified to V Chords

Basic Progression with ii–Vs Simplified to ii Chords

Principle #3: Emphasize Color Tones That Are Not Part of the Basic Key (Non-Diatonic)

As mentioned earlier, the chord tones that are not part of the basic key of the song often become the most distinctive part of the harmony. Mature improvisers seldom miss the opportunity to emphasize non-diatonic color tones by putting them on strong beats or preceding them with ornamentation. In many ways, this makes improvising on certain progressions much easier. Instead of having to worry about all the 3rds, 7ths, and altered tones of each chord, we can focus on the ones that are most expressive of the harmony (non-diatonic color tones). The etude on the next page has 31 chords but only 13 non-diatonic color tones. In the areas without a non-diatonic color tone, impovisers can easily create lyrical melodies in the main key of the song. Note: Being comfortable with a key still takes work. Practicing the all the scales and chords of a song's basic key should be part of the process before one starts to improvise.

Never Say Never

Ornamenting Non-Diatonic Color Tones (NDCT)

 Demonstration Tracks

Track 44 (Trumpet)

Track 45 (Tenor Saxophone)

Track 46 (Trombone)

Track 47 (Vocal)

Track 48 (Rhythm Track)

Never Say Never

Ornamenting Non-Diatonic Color Tones (NDCT)

C Treble Clef Instruments

Mike Steinel

NEVER SAY NEVER
Ornamenting Non-Diatonic Color Tones (NDCT)

Bb Instruments

Mike Steinel

Never Say Never

Ornamenting Non-Diatonic Color Tones (NDCT)

Eb Instruments

Mike Steinel

Never Say Never
Ornamenting Non-Diatonic Color Tones (NDCT)

C Bass Clef Instruments

Mike Steinel

Chapter 14: Using Altered Dominant Scales

Listen First

- Thelonious Monk: "Evidence" (Blue Note 1948)

- Michael Brecker: "What Is This Thing Called Love?" (*Merge*, Chiaroscuro, 1977; Jack Wilkins as Leader)

- Sonny Rollins and Miles Davis: "Airegin" (*Bags' Groove*, Prestige 1954)

- John Coltrane: "'Round Midnight" (*'Round About Midnight*, Columbia 1957)

Definitions

- **Altered Dominant**: A dominant chord with the 9th or the 5th lowered or raised (or the 13th lowered).

- **Tritone**: An augmented 5th or diminished 4th.

- **Tritone**: The interval between the 3rd and 7th of a dominant chord.

Dominant chords are perhaps the most powerful chords in jazz harmony. They introduce and sometimes extend the tension that makes their resolution satisfying to the listener. The tension in the dominant chord is produced by the tritone interval relationship between its 3rd and 7th. The 3rd and 7th of the dominant chord are the same notes as the 4th and 7th of the home key to which the dominant will resolve. Within the key, those notes are very unstable, and the musical ear will want them to move by step (up or down).

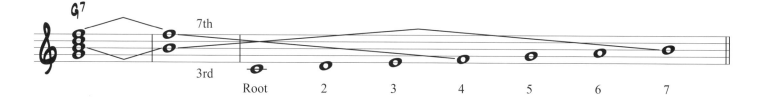

The tension introduce by the tritone (a diminished 5th or augmented 4th) is released when the interval becomes larger or smaller. When both voices expand, the notes resolve to the root and 3rd of the major I chord of the key. The same happens when the interval contracts (becomes smaller). This is the driving force of resolution in tonal music. The tritone needs to resolve.

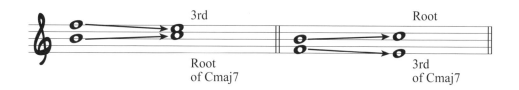

All dominant chords produce tension, but the tension is increased dramatically if altered notes are added. The root, 3rd, and 7th of a dominant cannot be altered since it will change the chord's basic dominant sound. Therefore, only the 9th, 5th, or 6th of a dominant can be altered. Altering those tones basically adds new tritones to the chord and creates added tension. There are four types of altered dominant chords: 1) dominants with altered 5ths; 2) dominants with altered 9ths; 3) dominants with altered 9ths and 13ths; and 4) dominants with altered 9ths and 5ths.

Four Types of Altered Dominant Chords

Dominants with Altered 5ths

Dominants with Altered 9ths

Dominants with Altered 9ths and 13ths

Dominants with Altered 9ths and 5ths

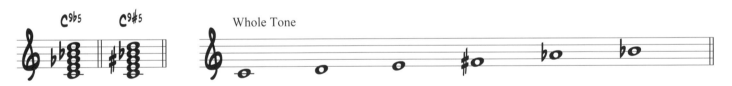

Each of these altered dominants have specific scales that contain the altered tones.

Dominants with Altered 5ths

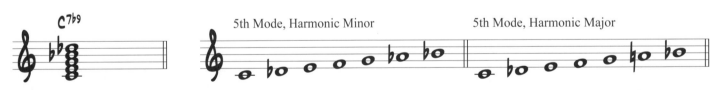

Dominants with ♭9ths

Dominants with Altered 9ths and 11ths

Dominants with Altered 13ths

Dominants with Altered 9ths and 13ths

Dominants with Altered 9ths and 5ths

Practice the following pattern from all 12 starting notes. The second bar of each pattern contains the chord the scale implies. Once you can play each scale (for memory) at a moderate tempo, experiment making melodies with the notes of each.

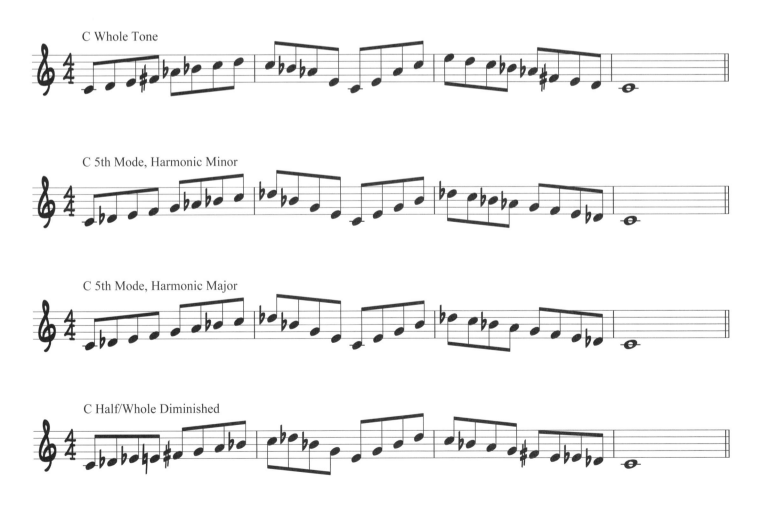

C Mixolydian ♭6

C Diminished/Whole Tone (7th Mode, Melodic Minor)

No More Questions

Using the Altered Dominant Scale and Modes

 Demonstration Tracks

Track 49 (Trumpet)

Track 50 (Tenor Saxophone)

Track 51 (Guitar)

Track 52 (Vocal)

Track 53 (Rhythm Track)

No More Questions

Using the Altered Dominant Scale and Modes

C Treble Clef Instruments

No More Questions
Using the Altered Dominant Scale and Modes

Bb Instruments

No More Questions

Using the Altered Dominant Scale and Modes

Eb Instruments

NO MORE QUESTIONS
Using the Altered Dominant Scale and Modes

C Bass Clef Instruments

Chapter 15: Using Pentatonic and Hexatonic Scales

Listen First

- John Coltrane: "Softly as in a Morning Sunrise" (*Live at the Village Vanguard*, Impulse 1961)

- Woody Shaw: "The Moontrane" (*Moontrane*, Muse 1974)

- Freddie Hubbard: "Red Clay" (*Red Clay*, CTI 1970)

- McCoy Tyner: "Passion Dance" (*Passion Dance*, Blue Note 1967)

- Michael Brecker: "What Is This Thing Called Love?" (*Merge*, Chiaroscuro 1977)

- Jerry Bergonzi: "It's the Same But..." (*The Line Between*, Whaling City Sounds 2013)

Definitions

- **Pentatonic Scale**: A five-note scale contained in one octave.

- **Major Pentatonic Scale**: 1, 2, 3, 5 and 6 of a major scale.

- **Minor Pentatonic Scale**: 1, ♭3, 4, 5, and ♭7 of a major scale (or 1, 3, 4, 5, and 7 of a minor scale).

- **Hexatonic Scale**: A six-note scale contained in one octave.

- **Intervallic Improvisation**: Jazz melody that uses wide intervals more than steps.

Pentatonics and Hexatonics in Jazz Improvisation

In the 1950s and 1960s, jazz musicians began to experiment with new melodic structures that would stand in contrast to the typical bebop melodies constructed using chord tone soloing and chromaticism. We learned in Chapter 9 that the use of scales and modes, which was part of the post-bop movement, generated a new melodic style that has been labeled as modal. The use of pentatonics and hexatonics generated another distinctively type of melody that is commonly referred to as **intervallic**. The structure of pentatonics and hexatonics lend themselves naturally to producing melodies that contain a limited number of 2nds. The pentatonic scale, in particular, will generate a large number of 4ths and 5ths.

Pentatonic Scales

Pentatonic scales have been part of many different musical cultures for centuries. There are numerous ways to divide the octave into five pitches, however the most common pentatonic, the major pentatonic, is built by using root, 2nd, 3rd, 5th, and 6th of a major scale. This configuration contains three whole steps and two minor 3rds.

C Major Scale

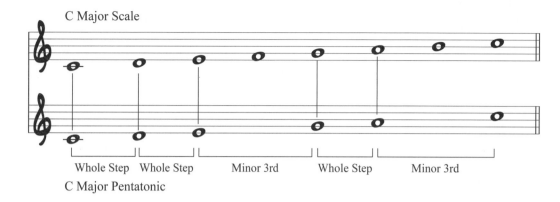

Because of its combination of steps and skips, the major pentatonic scale is a unique hybrid: part chord and part scale. It can easily produce the simple but lyrical melodies which are found in folk and pop music. Pentatonic melodies in jazz often have a unique sound, and because of the relationships in 4ths between their notes, they can generate textures that contrast dramatically with the tertian quality of chords built in 3rds. The basic major pentatonic scale generates six unique modes. The mode built on the fifth note is often called the minor pentatonic scale.

Modes of the C Major Pentatonic Scale

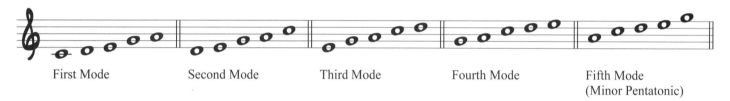

Most jazz chords contain the notes of at least one pentatonic scale. Those scales will "sound in unity," or consonant, with their related chord.

Major Pentatonic Scales That Sound Consonant with Common Chords

Chord   **Pentatonic Scales That Imply the Harmony**

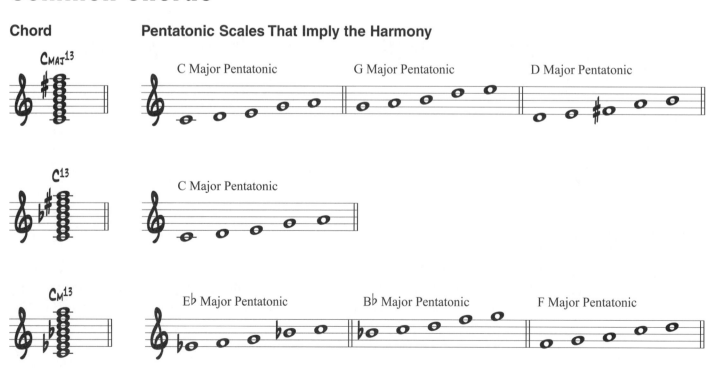

E♭ Major Pentatonic

G♭ Major Pentatonic

F Major Pentatonic   B♭ Major Pentatonic

Preliminary Exercises for the Major Pentatonic Scale

Practice these exercises from all 12 starting notes to gain facility in creating melodies using the major pentatonic scale.

Exercise 1

Exercise 2

Exercise 3

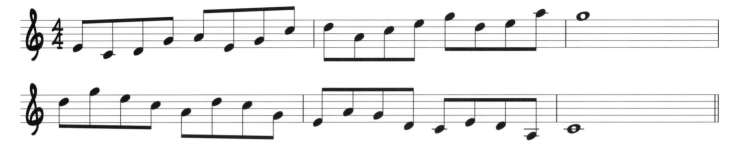

Hexatonics = Triad Pairs

In theory, any six-note scale could be considered a hexatonic; however, in practice, the most common hexatonic scales used in jazz are generally built by combining two triads that do not share any common tones. Every chord that generates a seven-note mode or scale will also contain a hexatonic triad pair. Some chord sounds will generate more than one option. Here are the most common triad pairs in jazz performance.

The Melodic Power of Triads and Pentatonics

The melodic strength and the distinct nature of triad and pentatonics cannot be overestimated. This certainly is the appeal of the triad and triad pairs for the modern jazz improvisers. The vocabulary of bebop-oriented jazz music is primarily made up of: 1) chords in 3rds, 2) scales in 2nds, and 3) chromatic ornamentations. Although pentatonics have major 2nds in their basic forms, in jazz performance, those are often avoided and melodies emphasize the more angular intervals (4ths and 5ths). Triads, because they are composed of 3rds and contain no 2nds, will seldom generate a scale-type melody.

Consonance vs. Dissonance

While pentatonics and hexatonics can be applied to achieve consonance, they can also be used to introduce dissonance. Dissonance can be a powerful attention-getting device in a solo. It should be noted that these dissonant passages are usually short and often preceded (and sometimes followed) by related thematic material that is more consonant. This is often referred to as "side slipping." Both triads and pentatonics are extremely effective in side slipping because their structures are harmonically unambiguous.

For more detailed information about pentatonics, consult *Pentatonic Scales for Improvisation* by Ramon Ricker and the *Inside Improvisation Series Vol. 2 – Pentatonics* by Jerry Bergonzi.

School's Out

Using Pentatonics and Hexatonics

 Demonstration Tracks

Track 54 (Trumpet)

Track 55 (Alto Saxophone)

Track 56 (Vocal)

Track 57 (Rhythm Track)

School's Out
Using Pentatonics and Hexatonics

C Treble Clef Instruments

Mike Steinel

School's Out
Using Pentatonics and Hexatonics

B♭ Instruments

Mike Steinel

School's Out
Using Pentatonics and Hexatonics

Eb Instruments

Mike Steinel

School's Out
Using Pentatonics and Hexatonics

C Bass Clef Instruments

Mike Steinel

Appendix

Thoughts on Post-Bop Change Running

Jazz began evolving in a variety of directions around the middle of the 20th century. Critics and audiences have assigned labels to the various streams of innovation as they appeared. After bebop, there was hard bop, West Coast jazz, cool, third stream, modal, free jazz, avant-garde, jazz rock, latin jazz, and acid jazz, to name a few. Perhaps the most accurate statement would be that jazz in the last 60 or 70 years has become eclectic. That is to say, it has been influenced by and mixed with a wide variety of musical styles that have changed the way modern improvisers deal with rhythm, harmony, form, and texture. Broad statements about the art form as is as it exists today are usually quickly challenged. However, at the risk of being rash or overly generalized, I would say that to a great extent, current jazz improvisations still involve the skill of change running. To be sure, the overall sonic effect may seem radically different than typical bebop soloing, but the goal of creating melodies that imply the harmony or relate to the harmony, what we call changes, is still a central feature in jazz soloing. There are two large differences. Over time, things have evolved: both the changes and the way modern jazz musicians relate to changes.

Important Changes in Jazz in the Post-Bop Era

- **Rhythm**: Eighth notes and triplets remained central, but players began incorporating odd rhythmic groupings. Quintuplets (five note groups) and septuplets (seven note groups) became more common.

- **Meter**: 4/4 remains the most common meter, but there has been significant experimentation into odd meters such as 7/8, 7/4, 5/4, etc.

- **Harmonic Density**: Particularly in the 1960s, composers such as Herbie Hancock, Wayne Shorter, and Miles Davis began emphasizing the use of complex altered harmonic structures.

- **Polychord Harmonies**: Once traditional tertian chords structures were pushed to their limit, some composers began inventing new structures by combining two or more chords.

- **Reharmonization**: Taking a cue from the bebop musicians of the 1940s like Charlie Parker, players and composers began adding new harmonic formulae to the traditional chord progressions from earlier eras.

- **Textures**: With the introduction of influences from rock music and the expanded use of electronic instruments, jazz musicians began to widen the textural palate available to them.

- **Free Elements**: In an effort to produce novel musical experiences, some musicians experimented with removing one or more of the basic elements of jazz performance. Harmony, form, and rhythm (the most pliable elements in jazz) were all candidates to be jettisoned in order to produce "free jazz."

- **Simpler Forms and Retro Jazz**: Many musicians have drawn upon earlier genres in reaction to rhythmic, harmonic, and formal elements have been pushed to their limit in post-bop jazz music.

Historical Perspective Is Important

It will be helpful to study the history of harmonic accuracy in jazz soloing from its earliest beginnings to the present day. The following chart contains two lines: The horizontal line indicates the actual harmony of jazz progressions while the diagonal line represents the harmonic content of jazz improvisations. The progression of time moves from left to right and starts circa 1910 and ends at 2010. Early jazz musicians typically created solos whose harmonic content was generalized, simple and at times and not related to the underlying harmony. At the far left of the chart, the diagonal line (solo content) is far away from the horizontal line (basic harmony). As jazz evolved, solos became less generalized, so the diagonal line moves a bit closer to the horizontal. But even the greatest solos of the Swing era by players like Lester Young seldom implied a complete picture of the harmony. In the Bebop era, the two lines begin to approach each other; however, even Charlie Parker neglected some chord changes.

There is a point where the two lines cross, and it coincides with the emergence of John Coltrane. Two albums stand as firm evidence of this phenomenon. The first is *Thelonious Monk and John Coltrane*. Recorded live at the Five Spot in 1957, Trane masterfully improvises on Monk's difficult songs by outlining nearly every chord. By contrast, Monk is far more generalized on his own material. Two years later, Coltrane recorded *Giant Steps*, an album that debuts a set of songs, some very fast, built on progressions that feature short chord lengths (two bars) and quick modulations between what were, at the time, unrelated keys. His solos on this album are extremely accurate, harmonically, and he never fails to outline each change. *Giant Steps* was a landmark recording, both for its compositional freshness and Coltrane's masterful execution.

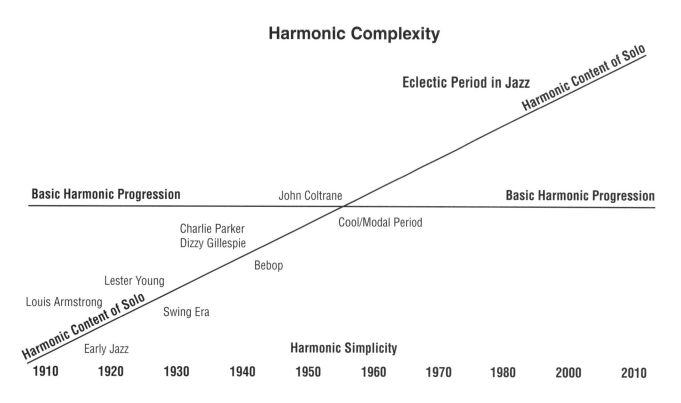

But the story doesn't end there. Trane continued evolving harmonically as he recorded 21 more albums before his death in 1967. On those recordings, he created melodies that had the same sort of harmonic complexity of *Giant Steps* (even more at times) but often seem to diverge from the given progressions of his compositions. If you look at the chart, after the lines cross, you see the harmonic content line move farther away from the horizontal. John Coltrane's influence on modern jazz improvisation is second to none, and perhaps his greatest impact is that in current jazz culture, improvisers are not only expected to imply changes of the harmony but they are expected to supply, at the least, moments when they imply more changes than the basic progression. We have been in the era of "extra harmony" in jazz for at least half a century.

Modern Devices Which Create "Extra Harmony"

Definitions

- **Chord Substitution**: The act of replacing a chord in a progression with another chord that is related. Basic chord substitution usually retains the general harmonic flavor of the progression.

- **Reharmonization**: The act of adding additional chords that purposely change the harmonic flavor of the original progression.

Chord Substitution

In the Bebop era, musicians like Charlie Parker and Dizzy Gillespie experimented by substituting new chords for the original chords. The most common were:

Upper Structure Substitution

Using the altered or unaltered 9ths, 11ths, or 13ths of the chord to build melodies. Often, this is achieved by substituting the given chord for a chord a 3rd or 5th away from the original.

Tritone Substitution

Substituting a dominant chord a tritone away from the given chord. Tritone subs are most accurately used between dominants but sometimes are used between other quality chords (usually through the device of chord quality change—see *Chord Quality Change*).

Back Door Substitution

Substituting a minor 7th based on the 4th of a key for the ii7 chord.

Reharmonization

Inserting Resolving Dominants

In principle, any chord can be preceded by a dominant chord a 4th below. Theorists term this process **tonicization**. In many cases, this will produce secondary dominants. Using altered versions of the added dominant increases the tension and the chromatic effect of the reharmonization.

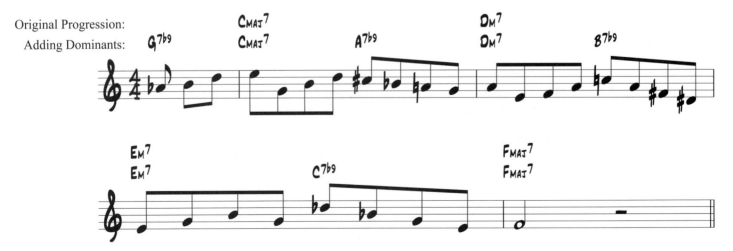

The Coltrane Matrix

This unique reharmonization is based on the relationship between keys that lie a major 3rd from each other. Coltrane began inserting it over the basic ii–V–I progression in standard tune progressions and later composed new compositions using "the Matrix" as original material.

Chord Quality Change

The quality of any chord can be changed to produce added harmonic tension. It is most common that major and minor chords are changed to dominants.

Scale/Mode Substitution

Substituting a different scale or mode for the scale or mode normally associated with a particular chord quality.

Motivic Chromaticism

Applying small bits of melody (**motifs**) randomly to various pitches to produce chromatic episodes. These are often determined by the improviser's basic intuition and retain their melodic integrity through the strength of the motifs rather than their harmonic accuracy. The motifs are commonly triads or fragments of pentatonic and bebop scales.

It would be impossible to document all the different devices used to produce "extra harmony" in jazz improvisations in the last 60 years, however the ones above are some that are quite common to the bulk of modern players. There are certainly some that are unique to individual performers and might defy any categorization. If you hear something you like in a solo transcribe it and do your own analyzation.

For a more complete discussion of the topic, I highly suggest David Liebman's *A Chromatic Approach to Jazz Harmony and Melody*, Bert Ligon's *Jazz Theory Resources*, and *Jazzology* by Robert Rawlins and Nor Eddine Bahha.

Practice Progressions

🔊 Practice Tracks

Track 58 [Major 7th Chords (All Keys)]

Track 59 [Dominant 7th Chords (All Keys)]

Track 60 [Minor 7th Chords (All Keys)]

Track 61 [ii–V–I Progressions (All Major Keys)]

Track 62 [ii–V–I Progressions (All Minor Keys)]

Practice Progressions: C Instruments

Major 7th Chords (All Keys)

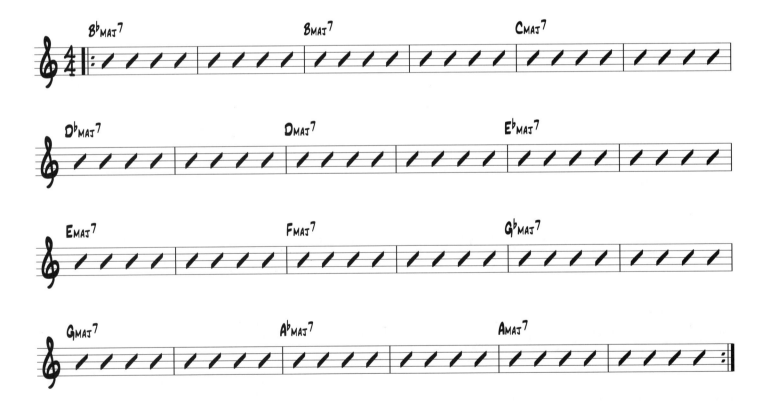

Dominant 7th Chords (All Keys)

Minor 7th Chords (All Keys)

ii–V–I Progressions (All Major Keys)

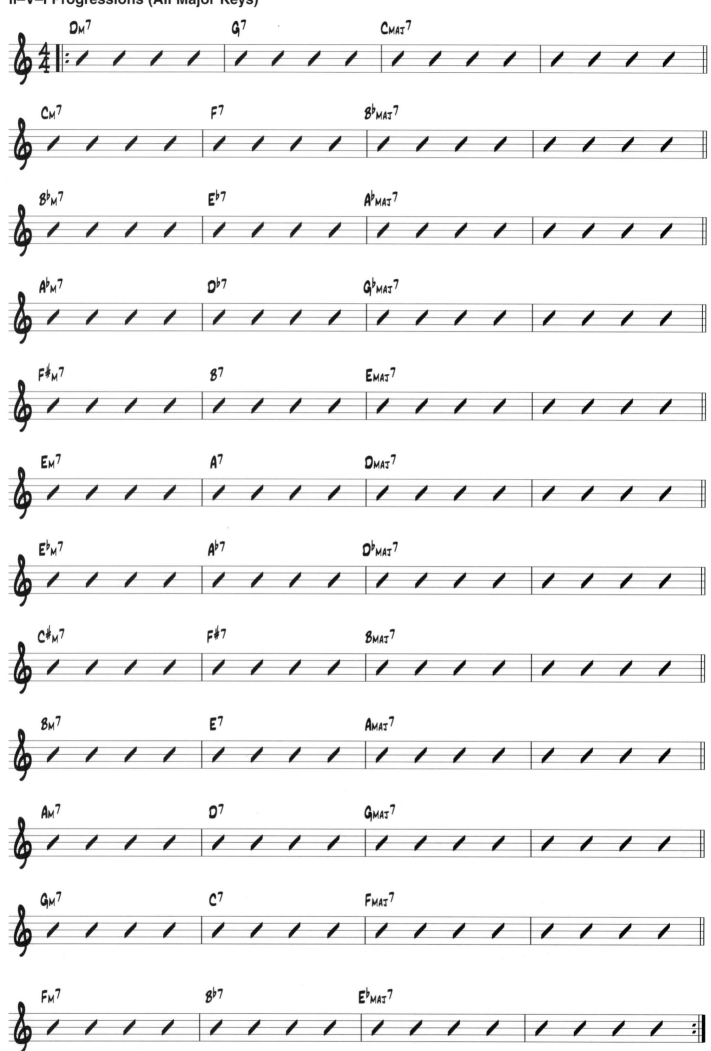

ii–V–I Progressions (All Minor Keys)

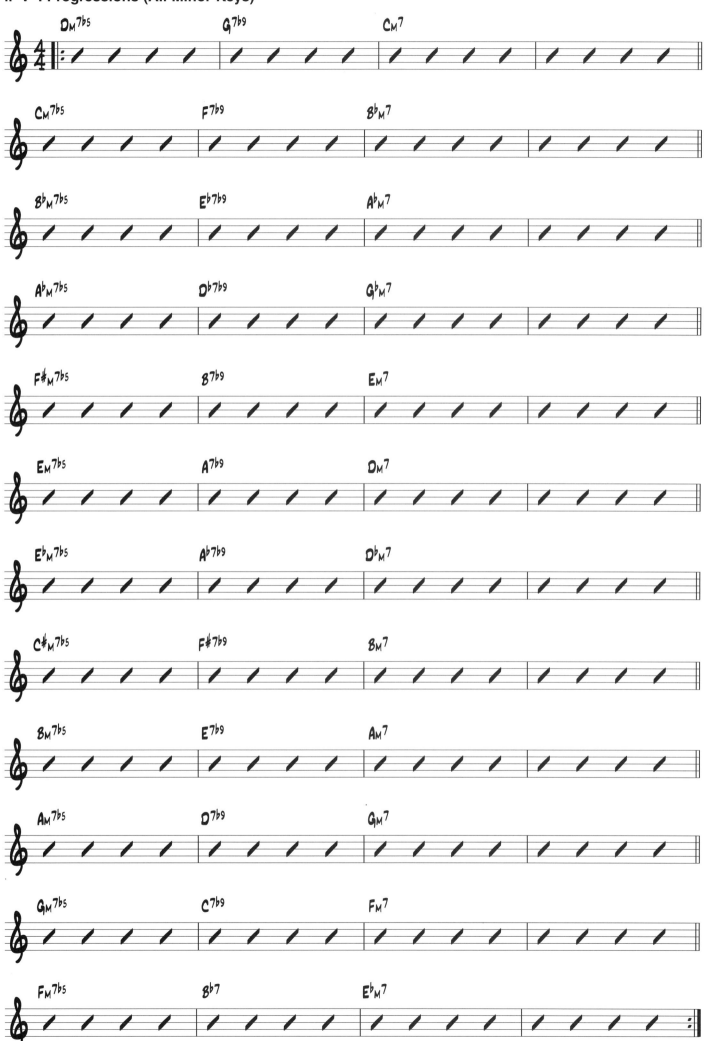

151

Practice Progressions: B♭ Instruments

Major 7th Chords (All Keys)

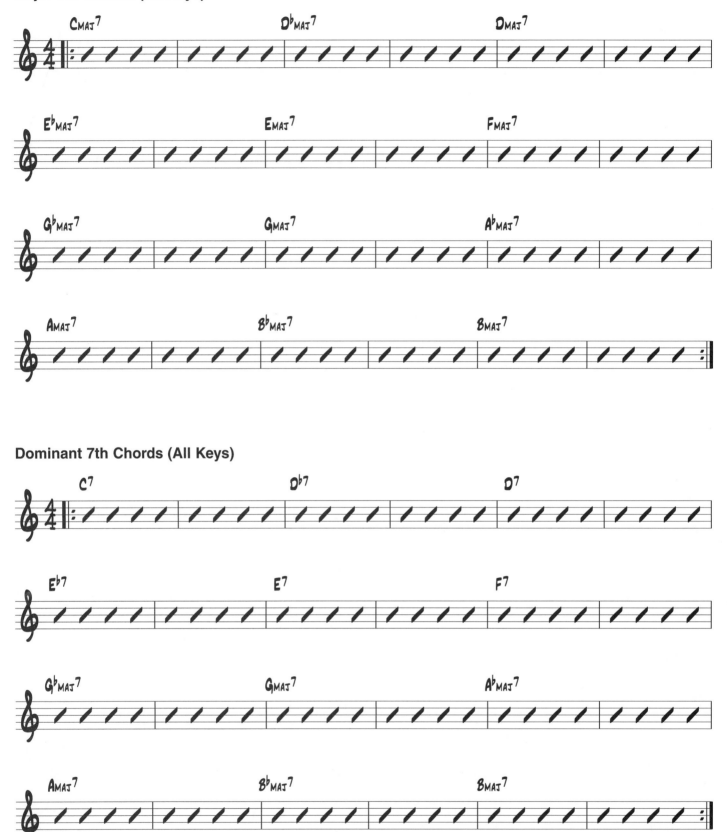

Dominant 7th Chords (All Keys)

Minor 7th Chords (All Keys)

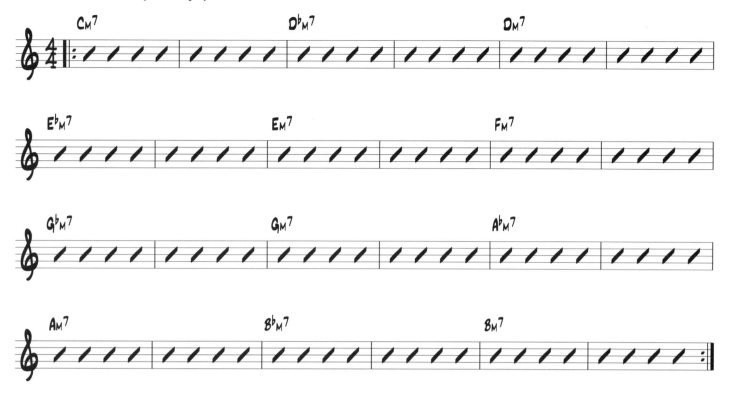

ii–V–I Progressions (All Major Keys)

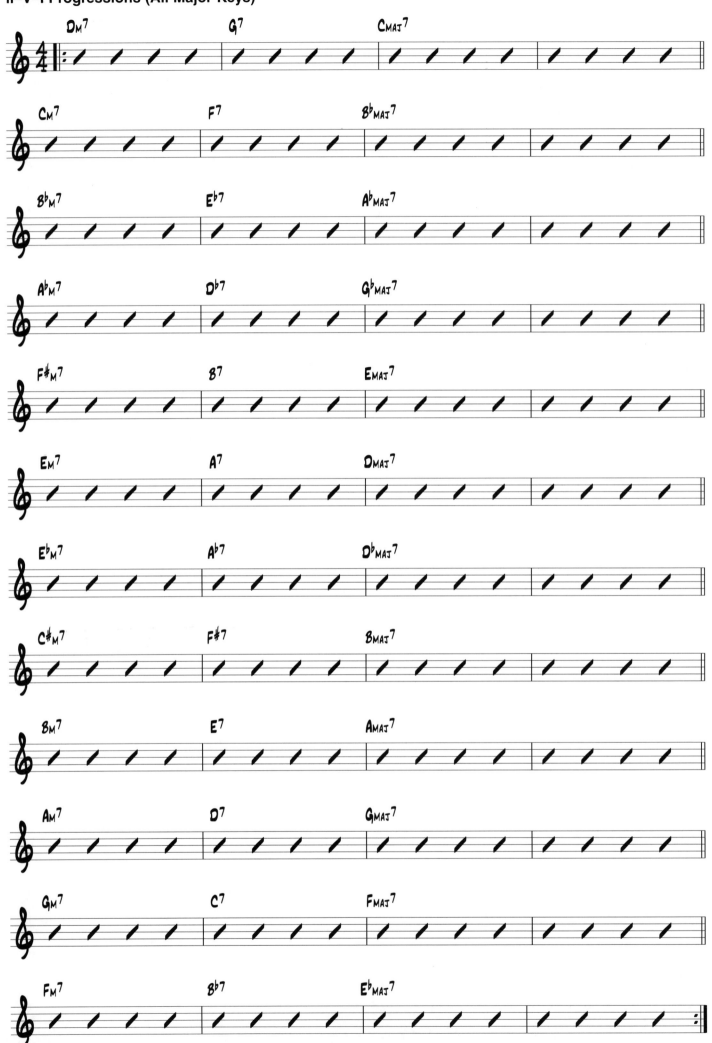

ii–V–I Progressions (All Minor Keys)

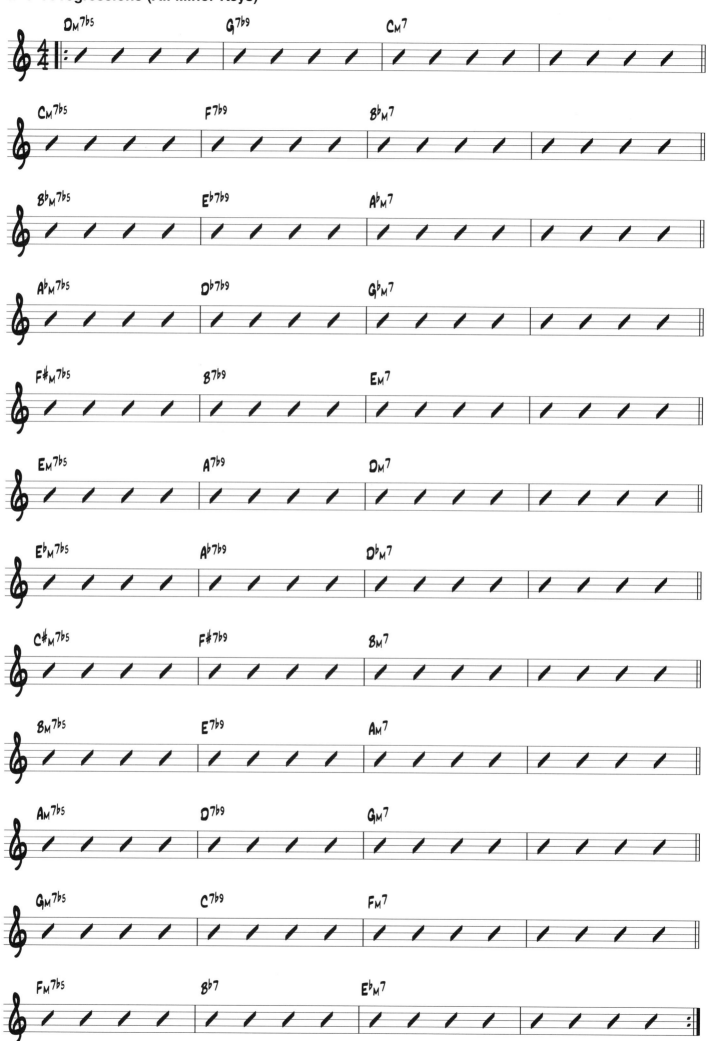

Practice Progressions: E♭ Instruments

Major 7th Chords (All Keys)

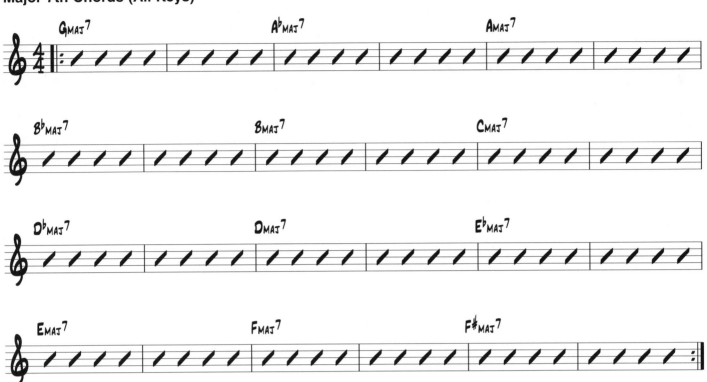

Dominant 7th Chords (All Keys)

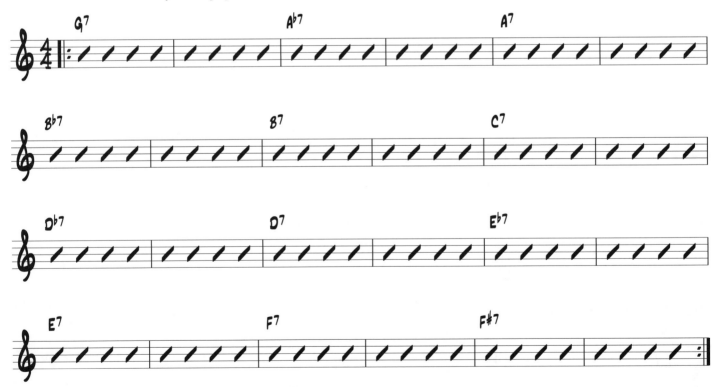

Minor 7th Chords (All Keys)

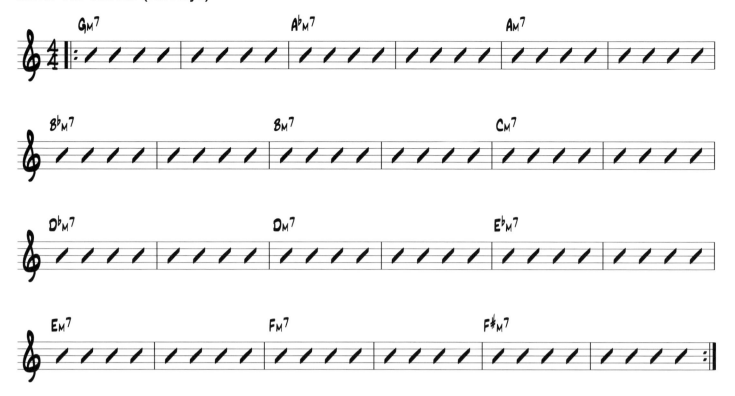

ii–V–I Progressions (All Major Keys)

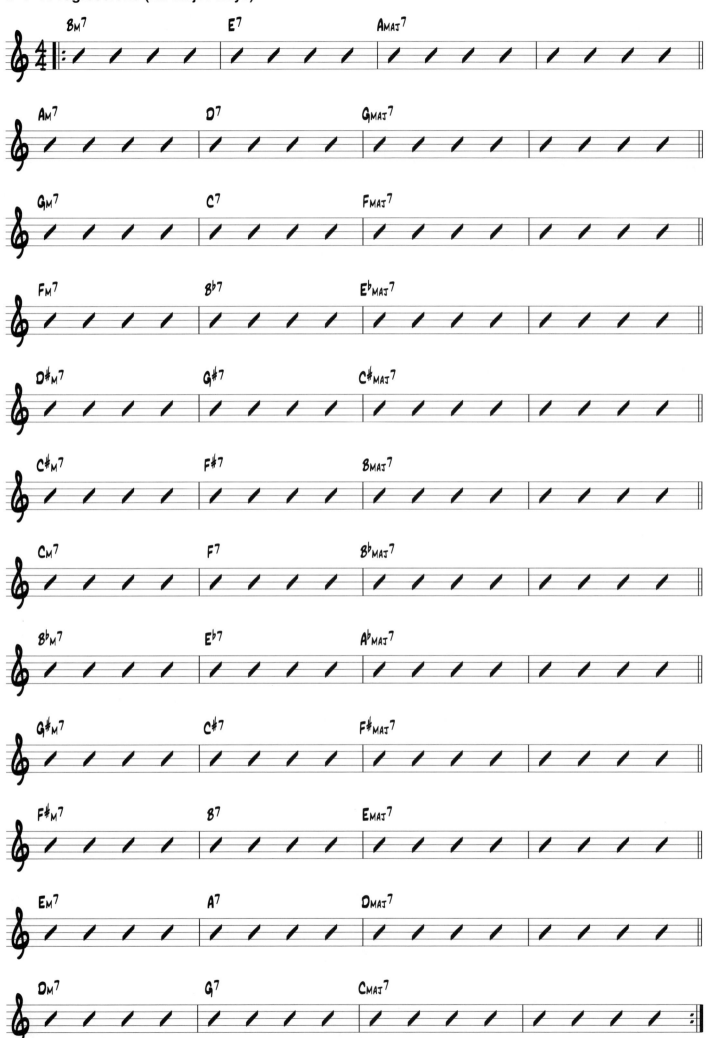

ii–V–I Progressions (All Minor Keys)

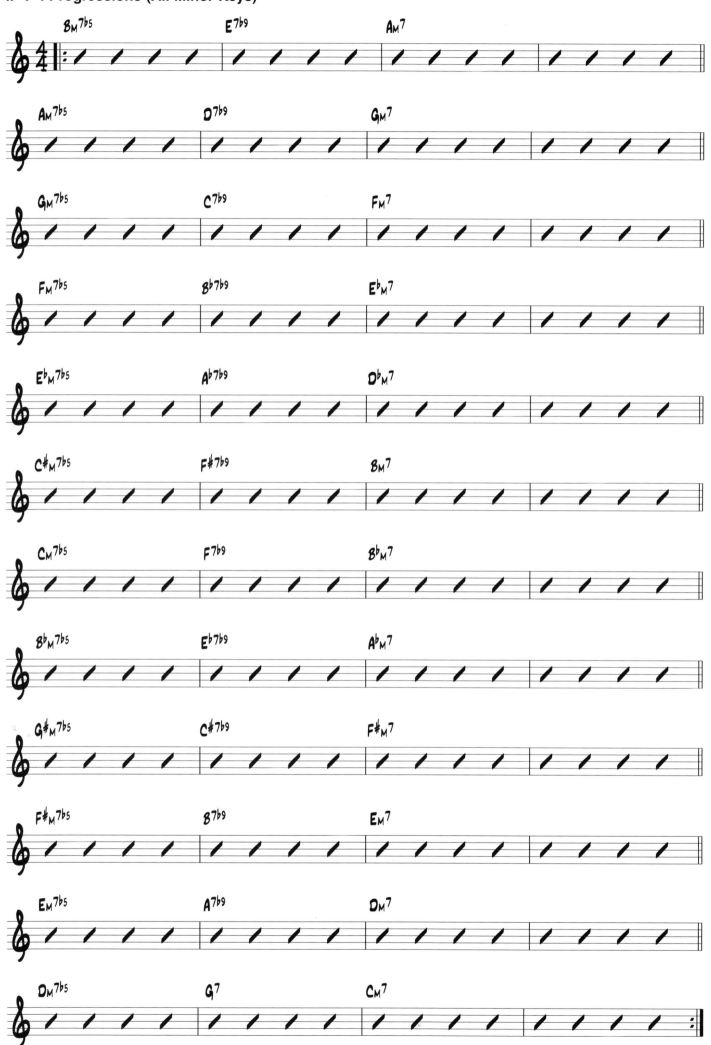

The Best-Selling Jazz Book of All Time Is Now Legal!

The Real Books are the most popular jazz books of all time. Since the 1970s, musicians have trusted these volumes to get them through every gig, night after night. The problem is that the books were illegally produced and distributed, without any regard to copyright law, or royalties paid to the composers who created these musical masterpieces.

Hal Leonard is very proud to present the first legitimate and legal editions of these books ever produced. You won't even notice the difference, other than all the notorious errors being fixed: the covers and typeface look the same, the song lists are nearly identical, and the price for our edition is even cheaper than the originals!

Every conscientious musician will appreciate that these books are now produced accurately and ethically, benefitting the songwriters that we owe for some of the greatest tunes of all time!

VOLUME 1

00240221	C Edition	$45.00
00240224	B♭ Edition	$45.00
00240225	E♭ Edition	$45.00
00240226	Bass Clef Edition	$45.00
00286389	F Edition	$39.99
00240292	C Edition 6 x 9	$39.99
00240339	B♭ Edition 6 x 9	$39.99
00147792	Bass Clef Edition 6 x 9	$39.99
00200984	Online Backing Tracks: Selections	$45.00
00110604	Book/USB Flash Drive Backing Tracks Pack	$85.00
00110599	USB Flash Drive Only	$50.00

VOLUME 2

00240222	C Edition	$45.00
00240227	B♭ Edition	$45.00
00240228	E♭ Edition	$45.00
00240229	Bass Clef Edition	$45.00
00240293	C Edition 6 x 9	$39.99
00125900	B♭ Edition 6 x 9	$39.99
00125900	The Real Book – Mini Edition	$39.99
00204126	Backing Tracks on USB Flash Drive	$50.00
00204131	C Edition – USB Flash Drive Pack	$85.00

VOLUME 3

00240233	C Edition	$45.00
00240284	B♭ Edition	$45.00
00240285	E♭ Edition	$45.00
00240286	Bass Clef Edition	$45.00
00240338	C Edition 6 x 9	$39.99

VOLUME 4

00240296	C Edition	$45.00
00103348	B♭ Edition	$45.00
00103349	E♭ Edition	$45.00
00103350	Bass Clef Edition	$45.00

VOLUME 5

00240349	C Edition	$45.00
00175278	B♭ Edition	$45.00
00175279	E♭ Edition	$45.00

VOLUME 6

00240534	C Edition	$45.00
00223637	E♭ Edition	$45.00

Also available:

00154230	The Real Bebop Book	$34.99
00240264	The Real Blues Book	$39.99
00310910	The Real Bluegrass Book	$39.99
00240223	The Real Broadway Book	$39.99
00240440	The Trane Book	$25.00
00125426	The Real Country Book	$45.00
00269721	The Real Miles Davis Book C Edition	$29.99
00269723	The Real Miles Davis Book B♭ Edition	$29.99
00240355	The Real Dixieland Book C Edition	$39.99
00294853	The Real Dixieland Book E♭ Edition	$39.99
00122335	The Real Dixieland Book B♭ Edition	$39.99
00240235	The Duke Ellington Real Book	$25.00
00240268	The Real Jazz Solos Book	$39.99
00240348	The Real Latin Book C Edition	$39.99
00127107	The Real Latin Book B♭ Edition	$39.99
00120809	The Pat Metheny Real Book C Edition	$34.99
00252119	The Pat Metheny Real Book B♭ Edition	$29.99
00240358	The Charlie Parker Real Book C Edition	$25.00
00275997	The Charlie Parker Real Book E♭ Edition	$25.00
00118324	The Real Pop Book – Vol. 1	$39.99
00240331	The Bud Powell Real Book	$25.00
00240437	The Real R&B Book C Edition	$45.00
00276590	The Real R&B Book B♭ Edition	$45.00
00240313	The Real Rock Book	$39.99
00240323	The Real Rock Book – Vol. 2	$39.99
00240359	The Real Tab Book	$39.99
00240317	The Real Worship Book	$35.00

THE REAL CHRISTMAS BOOK

00240306	C Edition	$35.00
00240345	B♭ Edition	$35.00
00240346	E♭ Edition	$35.00
00240347	Bass Clef Edition	$35.00
00240431	A-G CD Backing Tracks	$24.99
00240432	H-M CD Backing Tracks	$24.99
00240433	N-Y CD Backing Tracks	$24.99

THE REAL VOCAL BOOK

00240230	Volume 1 High Voice	$40.00
00240307	Volume 1 Low Voice	$40.00
00240231	Volume 2 High Voice	$39.99
00240308	Volume 2 Low Voice	$39.99
00240391	Volume 3 High Voice	$39.99
00240392	Volume 3 Low Voice	$39.99
00118318	Volume 4 High Voice	$39.99
00118319	Volume 4 Low Voice	$39.99

Complete song lists online at www.halleonard.com

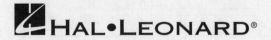

0422
318